Ordered 3-14-08

THE USE OF HISTORY

is the Key volume
in the

TEACH YOURSELF HISTORY
LIBRARY

Edited by **A. L. ROWSE**

Teach Yourself History

VOLUMES READY OR IN PREPARATION

THE
USE OF HISTORY

by

A. L. ROWSE
FELLOW OF ALL SOULS COLLEGE
OXFORD

Published by

HODDER & STOUGHTON LIMITED
for THE ENGLISH UNIVERSITIES PRESS
AT SAINT PAUL'S HOUSE
IN THE CITY OF LONDON

FIRST PRINTED . MAY 1946
SECOND IMPRESSION AUGUST 1946
THIRD IMPRESSION JUNE 1947
FOURTH IMPRESSION MARCH 1948

PRINTED IN GREAT BRITAIN FOR THE ENGLISH UNIVERSITIES PRESS, LTD.
LONDON, BY HAZELL, WATSON AND VINEY, LTD., LONDON AND AYLESBURY

A General Introduction to the Series

THIS series has been undertaken in the conviction that there can be no subject of study more important than history. Great as have been the conquests of natural science in our time —such that many think of ours as a scientific age *par excellence*—it is even more urgent and necessary that advances should be made in the social sciences, if we are to gain control of the forces of nature loosed upon us. The bed out of which all the social sciences spring is history; there they find, in greater or lesser degree, subject-matter and material, verification or contradiction.

There is no end to what we can learn from history, if only we will, for it is coterminous with life. Its special field is the life of man in society, and at every point we can learn vicariously from the experience of others before us in history.

To take one point only—the understanding of politics: how can we hope to understand the world of affairs around us if we do not know how it came to be what it is? How to understand Germany, or Soviet Russia, or the United States —or ourselves, without knowing something of their history?

v

8633

There is no subject that is more useful, or indeed indispensable.

Some evidence of the growing awareness of this may be seen in the immense increase in the interest of the reading public in history, and the much larger place the subject has come to take in education in our time.

This series has been planned to meet the needs and demands of a very wide public and of education—they are indeed the same. I am convinced that the most congenial, as well as the most concrete and practical, approach to history is the biographical, through the lives of the great men whose actions have been so much part of history, and whose careers in turn have been so moulded and formed by events.

The key idea of this series, and what distinguishes it from any other that has appeared, is the intention by way of a biography of a great man to open up a significant historical theme; for example, Cromwell and the Puritan Revolution, or Lenin and the Russian Revolution.

My hope is, in the end, as the series fills out and completes itself, by a sufficient number of biographies to cover whole periods and subjects in that way. To give you the history of the United States, for example, or the British Empire or France, *via* a number of biographies of their leading historical figures.

That should be something new, as well as convenient and practical, in education.

I need hardly say that I am a strong believer in people with good academic standards writing once more for the general reading public, and of the public being given the best that the universities can provide. From this point of view this series is intended to bring the university into the homes of the people.

A. L. ROWSE.

ALL SOULS COLLEGE,
  OXFORD.

TO

BRUCE McFARLANE

SCHOLAR, MENTOR, FRIEND

Contents

Contents

Preface

THE whole intention of this book is practical and didactic. It is designed as a statement of the case for the study of history, a discussion of its uses and pleasures and as a manual of instruction on how to approach the subject.

But though my object has been practical at every point, an historian cannot write a book saying what he really thinks about his subject without developing some general reflections and going into some abstract questions. These are mainly concentrated in Chapter V. If the reader finds that chapter too uncongenial on a first reading, he should skip it, go on to the end and then return to it at his leisure. Since it contains the essence of what I have to contribute on a difficult and important subject, perhaps I may be forgiven for suggesting a second reading.

Short as this book is, it incorporates the experience of many years' teaching and lecturing, thinking and writing about the subject. I cannot express what I owe to friends and colleagues at Oxford with whom I have discussed many of the points that are pronounced upon here, I hope not too summarily.

A. L. ROWSE.

OXFORD,
   Michaelmas, 1945.

Chapter One

What is the Use of History?

WHEN I was a boy at school a question that was frequently asked was: *What is the use of history?* And nobody seemed to have any answer. (If the school had been somewhat better, the answer would have been forthcoming all right; for, as I hope to show you, there is a completely satisfactory answer to the question, an overwhelming case for the study of history.)

Nobody had any doubt about the use of science: its utility was stamped upon the face of the subject. You could become a chemist or a physicist or an engineer. But could you become an historian? Even if you could, what did it lead to?

These were no doubt very inadequate modes of thinking; we were only boys at a very remote provincial secondary school. But some such modes of thought are current much more widely, if not generally in the modern world. And what we meant by 'use' was, mainly if not wholly, what use is studying history as a preparation for a career? What kind of job does it lead to? There is a good deal more in the question than that, of course. But even to take it at its most practical and utilitarian, the advantages are by no means so wholly on the side of science as we thought in those days.

Privately, and for myself alone, I very much doubted the use of the weary hours I spent in the physics and chemistry laboratories: what was the use, I thought, of making those horrid smells, of weighing those refractorily ponderable substances, of memorising those innumerable formulæ? Of course, I was wrong. For other lads there was some use, and even pleasure, in it. And yet, years afterwards, in a very progressive and sympathetic little book on the teaching of science, I find the authors questioning whether there is much educational value in teaching chemistry in schools. I thought as much years ago—was my reflection on reading that.

And yet—joking apart—we do not need to question the general use of science and its study for a moment. We are only too well aware of its necessity in an industrial civilisation. And beyond the mere question of its utility, in a more profound sense, so far from being anti-science, I am all on the side of the whole scientific movement of thought which, from the Renaissance onwards, has come to characterise and dominate the intellect of the modern world. History is not in conflict with it; in the course of the nineteenth century it became part of it. The emergence of the concept of evolution into a central position in thought equally affected science and history, and—what is a more original reflection—provided a ground of junction between the two. It is sufficiently realised that the methods of evolutionary science affected the study of history; what is not so well grasped is that with the theory of evolution history may be said to have permeated the whole conception of science. This interaction, which had such an extraordinary fertilising influence upon nineteenth-century thought —so much so as to give it its dominating character —has a still more fruitful career before it, if only we can do our duty by the intellectual needs of our time with some new thinking, instead of dressing up in a new clothing some of the most outworn categories of medieval thought—such as, for example, the essentially debased character of human nature, the original stain that lies upon it, etc.: clichés which have a temporarily revived *réclame* in time of war and whose exploitation is all the more vulgar because its success comes from the pain and suffering abroad at such a time.

We are all familiar with the popular slogan that this is a scientific age, but people are not so well aware that, in a profound sense, it is no less an historically-minded age.

These are important themes and they will have their place later on in this book. I cannot expound them now; I only wish to point out that, in spite of the extreme importance of history for the intellectual outlook of our time, we are in general much less conscious of the need and use

3

of history ordinarily than we are of that of science. Then I wish to return to the most severely practical, and indeed utilitarian, approach to the subject.

History has its uses from the point of view of a career, getting a job—apart from anything else it may offer—no less than science; and these uses may throw some further light on the value of the subject in and for itself.

Let us start with education, with that decisive stage in its progress the transition from school to university, from adolescent to adult life. (We shall deal with history in schools later.) A large number of history scholarships to the university are awarded; they form a major category of scholarships at Oxford and Cambridge: so that history gives you an open door, if ingress is necessarily limited, to the university and an academical career. Afterwards there are the openings for properly equipped teachers of the subject in colleges and schools of all kinds—there must be some thousands of such teachers. Around the teaching profession there are certain cultural posts, librarians, archivists, curators of museums, secretaries of institutions, social service workers—not many in all, but definitely on the increase with the social trends of our time. A more important profession is journalism, with which we may include broadcasting. For political journalists, foreign and military correspondents, it is a great advantage to have had an historical

4

education: so many of the affairs they have to deal with need just that background in order to understand them and make them clear. It is not without significance that some of the most powerful journalists of our time, men who have a large part in forming intelligent opinion on public affairs—such men as 'Scrutator' of the *Sunday Times*, the chief leader-writer on international affairs on the *Times*, 'Candidus' of the *Daily Sketch* and elsewhere—are historically trained minds: two of them are distinguished historians in their own right and the third has the passion of a *dévot* for the subject. Nor is it surprising that such noted publicists as Sir Ernest Barker, Arthur Bryant, D. W. Brogan, Professor Laski all have a background of historical study. Their comments would be of less weight if they had not.

Even more important, there is the Civil Service. History is one of the recognised roads into its higher ranks; it is an important subject in the entrance examination. And it might quite rightly have greater influence attached to it; for history gives you the right background for most of the affairs with which you will have to deal in the administrative Civil Service. I remember a Civil Service Commissioner, who was in the best position to know, confiding to me how hopeless as an administrator a Cambridge mathematician was apt to be. That is only natural: one would expect him to be much better placed in some scientific profession or research post.

5

The work of the Civil Service is for the most part concerned with nothing so pure and abstract as mathematics, but with the administration of human affairs, with the social sciences if you like —for which the appropriate background and training are provided by history. (Again it is significant that three of the greatest civil servants of our time—Sir Robert Morant, Sir William Beveridge, Sir Arthur Salter—read Greats subjects at Oxford or the school of *Literæ Humaniores*. Today they would probably have read History or Modern Greats. Sir Horace Wilson, that name of ill-omen, seems to have been educated at the London School of Economics. It was very clear that he did not know the history of modern Europe.)

If history is the appropriate training on the whole for civil servants, it follows that it is indispensable for members of the foreign service, for diplomats and consuls abroad. In all the pitiable revelation of a third-rate mind in a front-rank post that is afforded by a reading of Sir Nevile Henderson's *Failure of a Mission*—he was in a key position as British Ambassador in Berlin from 1937 to 1939—nothing is more deplorable than the ignorance of the man as to the character of the developments in Germany. Only a little orderly reading of modern German history would have given him the clue to them. But he seems to have thought a reading of *Mein Kampf* on board ship from South America home was

6

sufficient. No wonder he was both fogged and foxed by the direction of events in Germany and seems never to have grasped it until too late. Nor was he the only one to whom a little knowledge of German history would have brought a world of enlightenment. How can one properly understand the career of Hitler and the resurgence of German militarism, its undying appeal for the German people, if one knows nothing of Bismarck and Frederick the Great, of the whole cult of militarism, the tradition of German aggression? Sir Eyre Crowe at the head of our Foreign Office before the last war understood these things very well; and that is why his formulation of the exigencies of British policy was far more cogent and foreseeing than any subsequent statement of our policy between the two wars. A clearer and more informed view of the situation and its developments might have prevented a second war.

It ought not to have been so very difficult to forecast, on quite a moderate acquaintance with the German people and their recent history, that they would make a second bid for world-power. The worst thing that their history reveals, worse than their criminal brutality, their stupidity and insensibility, their sycophancy and self-pity, is their utter lack of any sense of responsibility for what they do—for that is what leads to all the rest. When I lived in Germany for a winter after the last war, in a 'good' middle-class household, that of a Lutheran pastor—at a time when we in this country were already beginning to sit superfluously in a white sheet for a responsibility that was not ours—I never heard one word of regret for the war they had precipitated upon the world, with its untold losses in men's lives. All that they regretted was that they had lost it: they were incapable of seeing anything beyond that. And I gather from all that I hear and read, and from what I know of them, that even after this second war they loosed upon the world, they have still not learnt the simple lesson—that war is not a good thing, but merely that it is a bad thing to lose a war. There is no sign, I am assured, that they recognise any responsibility for what has happened.

That absence of a sense of responsibility, the necessary foundation of any civic sense, runs right through German life from top to bottom and reflects their history. It is the most danger-ous thing of all, the source of all their misdeeds and misfortunes, for it means a people with great powers of organisation and endurance and of brutal strength, but with no moral courage : they are therefore always at the service of any masters who are prepared to drive them forward along the road of aggression to power. Power is the inducement; power is what they worship: they have no notion that there is anything else that exists in the world of politics. And aggression is the method. After all, aggression is what has always paid in German history. Frederick the

8

Great's career was one long record of successful aggression. So was Bismarck's. The total upshot of Bismarck's irruption upon the scene was to put back the clock a hundred years in European civilisation. But the Germans have no sense of that: he did well for Germany, so they thought— and still think, according to Karl Barth, in spite of the immense catastrophe that was the ultimate consequence of his life's work. Yet Frederick and Bismarck are the two great heroes of politics to the German mind—and likely to remain so. *Achtung!* The Germans are never likely to change until they get those two out of their minds, rid their system of them.

It was not really to be supposed that when the culmination of decades of successful aggression came with their bid for world-power in 1914–1918, which so nearly came off and was only scotched in the end, they would not make a second and bigger effort. All the elements in Germany that stood to gain by it were in the conspiracy: the old Junker militarist classes, the landowners, the armaments manufacturers, the big industrialists, large elements of the middle classes and their unhappy stooges in an idiot peasantry, and the *déclassés* of all types and sections. We received ample warning of what would happen: it was in the books. It was written in plenty of books: I read a great many of them myself and knew quite well what to expect. There is an ample literature on the history of modern Germany: there is really

9

no excuse for not knowing. But what was so sickening in the years before the war was that none of them seemed to have been read by people in high place, responsible for the conduct of our affairs. It is indispensable that they should know something of the history of modern Europe.

If this is true of the diplomatic service—and it is there an obvious and urgent necessity—it is no less so for our political leadership, of which the Higher Civil Service has become part. We simply cannot afford as a nation a political leadership which is ignorant of the facts, and the trends, of modern European and world history.

Ignorance in high places, and in particular the absence of any historical understanding of the political developments in Europe, led us in the last ten years as near as anything to disaster. It is all very well for the circles mainly responsible to blame it now, with a kind of mean generosity, upon the people at large. The people were no doubt ignorant: they always are. But that is no reason why they should continue to be so. (It is the main purpose of such a series of books as this to dispel ignorance, in so far as it can.) I agree with one of the first and greatest of Englishmen, King Alfred, that there is nothing more dangerous than ignorance: as he wrote at the end of his life more than a thousand years ago: "I know nothing worse of a man than that he should not know." How right he was! The trouble with human beings has always been not that they ate of the

Tree of Knowledge but that they did not eat enough of it.

After two disastrous decades in which the dominant figures in English politics were two Midlands industrialists, what a relief it was to have an historian as Prime Minister. And in spite of what all the mediocrities thought, how much safer! For, as an historian, Mr. Churchill knew the underlying long-term exigencies of British policy, the interests of ourselves and the Empire without which we cannot exist. He has them in his bones: they are indeed, one might almost say, in his heredity; for has not Mr. Churchill performed for us in our time precisely what his great ancestor, Marlborough, achieved for us in his?

Take the case of the policy of the Grand Alliance. That has been the dominating, as it was the necessary, pattern of our policy throughout our modern history; when we departed from it we risked, and sometimes experienced, disaster; when we adhered to it we were successful: we were safe, and others along with us. What it means is that when some aggressive power in Europe, Philip II's Spain, the France of Louis XIV and Napoleon, the Germany of William II and Hitler—has become so powerful as to challenge our safety and sometimes the very existence of others, we have banded together with those others in a common alliance to defend ourselves against the overwhelmingly powerful aggressor.

What more natural and right? It is only common sense. It is just what a number of smaller boys would do at school to resist the tyrannies of a bully.

Yet it is extraordinary how that policy—simple and right as it is, in our own interest as well as that of the bulk of other peoples—has been misunderstood and reviled. One can understand the misrepresentations of this policy, and the dislike of its success by some continental historians, a Debidour or a Treitschke—because it defeated the aggressive game of their own particular country, with which they identified themselves. They always put down our success in forming continental coalitions to Machiavellianism and English gold. It is really very simple and naïf of them; their jealousy blinds their judgment. For with all the Machiavellianism and gold in the world it would have been impossible to form these coalitions, if it had not been in the interest of other peoples as well as ourselves. As a matter of fact, it has usually been even more in other peoples' interest than our own.

Consider this: as against Philip II and Louis XIV our security was threatened, but hardly our very existence as a nation. That of Holland was. Again with Napoleon, as an island we were in a stronger position than other powers; the very independence of most powers of Western Europe was at stake. In our own time, against Germany, our danger has been greater; but not greater than the mortal danger in which France, Poland, Russia, Norway, Denmark, Holland, Belgium, and all Central and Southern Europe have stood. The fact is that we have a common interest with the great bulk of Europe against an aggressor so powerful as to threaten us all; and that has been the sheet-anchor of our security as a nation in modern times.

It can hardly be a legitimate matter of complaint that this has been very much to our interest. If a power goes clean contrary to its interest it comes to disaster. What is more to the point is that our interest has been compatible with the interest of others, i.e. with the general interest.

Consider too what it has safeguarded: the cultural variety, the astonishing creative fertility and freedom of Europe. If it had not been for us there might have been a succession of uniform patterns imposed by repressive hegemonies upon Europe. We have kept the way open for the infinitely varied contributions of the smaller, less powerful countries to the wonderful creative amalgam that is European culture. There was a time, not long ago, when some Frenchmen regretted our resistance to Napoleon's domination of Europe; they now have had more reason to welcome our resistance to Hitler's. Nor is our historic resistance to continental tyranny ultimately to be regretted by those great powers themselves which have tried to exercise it. Na-

13

poleon's immense efforts only exhausted France, and while they were going on they were culturally sterilising. The deliverance of France from his bondage was followed by a century of the most wonderful achievement in the arts that even France has known. And perhaps the deliverance of Germany from the nightmare of aggressive militarism may have a similar effect of release in the sphere of culture and the spirit.

In fact, though few people seem to realise it, our rôle has been a decisive one in the making of modern Europe, apart from its effect upon the outer world, of which people are more aware. And it has been sufficiently misrepresented abroad, without our depreciating it and misunderstanding it here.

Of all this that is involved in the policy of the Grand Alliance, of its necessity for us and the consequences that flow from it, Mr. Churchill had a firm grasp that was rooted in history. It was not that he saw the point *ex post facto*—after the facts of the situation had forced us back to the old sound tradition of our policy. He saw it all before: his speeches throughout the decade in which we wandered away from it are full of that theme. And it is interesting that it was just during those same years that he was writing his historical masterpiece, *Marlborough: His Life and Times*. Marlborough was the linch-pin of the Grand Alliance that defeated the aggressive designs of Louis XIV and ended his domination in

Europe: he was not only its military leader (the greatest soldier in our history) but its brain-centre, its chief diplomatic and executive agent. The career of his ancestor not only affords us a parallel to Mr. Churchill's rôle in defeating Hitler, but it has been a direct influence upon him in performing it.

And how much we owe to him because of it! When the history of this war comes to be written it may well be that an even greater service, if possible, than his part in serving his country in 1940 was that which he rendered in helping to bring into being the great alliance by which alone the Fascist Powers in Europe and the Far East could be defeated. It was because of this background of thought that he was ready to respond to Hitler's invasion of Soviet Russia with an immediate offer of mutual aid and alliance.

The danger of knowing no history can be brought home even more sharply and simply than over this question of the Grand Alliance. Take the issue of what was happening in Germany in the past ten years, and what was to be expected. Many of our political leaders, and leaders of public opinion, simply did not know what to expect. Mr. Churchill knew very well what to expect, though he could not get the people responsible to believe him in time. But then he was a student of history: he had been there before.

Mr. Churchill's case provides us with the

strongest possible argument for an historical education. He educated himself by studying history; he formed his mind upon it; in the end he became an historian, and wrote one of the finest works of historical scholarship in our time. It is an interesting story: you will find his account of it in his autobiography, *My Early Life*.[1]

You will already have guessed what I think to be the prime—though not the only—use of history. It is that it enables you to understand, better than any other discipline, the public events, affairs and trends of your time. What could be more important? If you do not understand the world you live in, you are merely its sport, and apt to become its victim. (Most people are that anyway. But that is no reason why you should be one of them. In understanding is our only emancipation.)

For that is what history is about. It is about human society, its story and how it has come to be what it is; knowing what societies have been like in the past and their evolution will give you the clue to the factors that operate in them, the currents and forces that move them, the motives and conflicts, both general and personal, that shape events. It is a study in which you are dealing with human nature all the time; that is where the biographies of great historic figures come in and why it is so useful (besides being very pleasant) to read them.

[1] And cf. my essay, "Mr. Churchill and English History," in *The English Spirit*.

16

But history deals not only with the lives of great individuals; in a sense it may be said to consist of the sediment of the lives of millions of smaller men and women who have left no name, but who have made their contribution. Their lives make the material of history as a coral-reef is built up out of the lives of millions of molluscs.

History is then a social science. In that lies its flexibility, its variety and excitement. It is so much less rigid than physical science, so much more subtle and appealing to the imagination, for it deals with human beings in all their complexity and incalculability. It is always alive and can be thrilling.

But that does not mean that you cannot draw lessons or form generalisations from it. Of course you can, as from ordinary human experience. Only with history you have so much more range of experience to draw upon: in fact the whole range of human experience we know of. And though the individual is apt to be unpredictable (even he is not always), great social groupings, masses of men, classes, communities, nations tend to react in similar ways to similar situations. They give you the ground of history, so to say—the stuff upon which the more intricate and individual patterns have been worked. And so, though you may hardly say that there are historical laws of the regularity and exactness of the laws of physical science, there are generalisations possible, of something like a statistical character. There is no need for a chaotic scepticism with regard to history. The fact that such generalisations and tendencies are more irregular, the movements more complex, is all the more intellectually exciting because of their subtlety. You are dealing all the time with human material; so that you need above all common sense, sympathy, imagination to appreciate and understand it.

It is public affairs, public events and movements that give you the indispensable background. That is the truth expressed in the much-discussed dictum of Seeley, "History is past politics; politics is present history." It is not that Seeley's saying is untrue—though it is sometimes attacked as if it were; but that it is not exhaustive. It is indeed very inadequate; there is so much else in history, as there is in the human experience that is history, besides politics or even social affairs. But all the same, society and its affairs give you the pattern.

Now you will see why I think history is of the utmost importance at the universities, as a preparation for the teaching profession, the Civil Service, our political leadership in its widest sense, leaders of the press and public opinion, no less than for politicians. A knowledge of history is indispensable to the higher direction of society; that is why it is especially important in higher education, and the higher up the more important.

There is a popular saying that 'history never repeats itself'; and that is sometimes given as a

18

reason for holding that you cannot draw lessons from it. Of course it does not repeat itself in exact detail, for there are never the same persons, the same situations with precisely the same characters again. But that does not mean that there are not similar situations, which similarly handled lead to similar results. Over and over again one notices in the history of revolutions—to take one example—the same kind of crisis crop up, a situation with very much the same elements constituting it, whether it is England in the 1640's, France in the 1790's, or the Russia of 1917; one sees the situation ill understood and worse handled by an old régime feebly directed, whether by Charles I, Louis XVI, or Nicholas II, and the situation get out of hand in much the same manner. It is a point that is made, perhaps too dogmatically—as if almost there were a natural history of revolution—by Trotsky in his *History of the Russian Revolution*. But the general point holds good.

H. A. L. Fisher after spending some years in writing his *History of Europe*, summed up his view of it in his Preface: "One intellectual excitement has, however, been denied me. Men wiser and more learned than I have discovered in history a plot, a rhythm, a predetermined pattern. These harmonies are concealed from me. I can see only one emergency following upon another as wave follows upon wave, only one great fact with respect to which, since it is unique, there can be no generalisations, only one safe rule for the historian: that he should recognise in the development of human destinies the play of the contingent and the unforeseen. This is not a doctrine of cynicism and despair. The fact of progress is written plain and large on the page of history; but progress is not a law of nature. The ground gained by one generation may be lost by the next. The thoughts of men may flow into the channels which lead to disaster and barbarism."

There is a lot of disillusioned Liberalism in that. We need not cavil at the latter half of what Fisher says. But with regard to the first: there is of course no *one* rhythm, or *one* plot in history. To suppose that there is, or even to expect it and be disappointed, is a relic of the religious view of the universe with its providential ordering of history to a given *terminus ad quem*. Acton's somewhat unilateral view of history as the unfolding story of human freedom—a view very characteristic of the nineteenth century—is in direct line of descent from Bossuet's teleological view of Universal History as leading up to the Christian revelation; and paradoxically enough, is in direct line coming from St. Augustine, whose emphasis was yet quite contrary to human freedom.

No: there is no one rhythm or plot in history, but there are rhythms, plots, patterns, even repetitions. So that it is possible to make generalisations and to draw lessons. Great men both of action and of intellect have always thought so.

That is why history was the favourite reading of Napoleon, as of Lloyd George and Mr. Churchill —or for that matter, of Hitler. (He might with advantage have read a little more clearly Napoleon's campaign of 1812 in Russia. But then Hitler was a profoundly *uneducated* man of genius: there could be nothing more dangerous, with such a criminal mentality in a position of power.) All the ancients, both Greek and Roman, read history not only for pleasure, but for the light it threw upon events and the lessons they could learn from it. So too with the men of the Renaissance: Machiavelli, Erasmus, Thomas More, Bodin, Guicciardini, Bacon, Hobbes, Clarendon. Sir Charles Firth tells us: "Not only is it a branch of learning to be studied for its own sake, but a kind of knowledge which is useful to men in daily life," and he quotes Sir Walter Ralegh, "the end and scope of all history being to teach us by example of times past such wisdom as may guide our desires and actions." This it is that makes Bacon say when discussing the virtues of different kinds of studies: "Histories make men wise."

What kind of lessons are those that history teaches ? you may ask. They are indeed innumerable, and of all kinds, personal as well as social. But we are confining ourselves to the more strictly political, the realm in which a knowledge of history is a prime necessity.

Let us take, for example, the truth expressed in the saying that you may expel history with a

pitchfork but it always comes back. How revealing that is of the course of revolutions: you may
see it at work in each of the three great revolutions I have mentioned, the English, the French
and the Russian. With the execution of Charles I,
Cromwell and his Army made a drastic break
with the English past, they scrapped the old
monarchical form of government that was
deeply entrenched in our experience. But it was
not long before monarchy came sweeping back
again; a few years before, Cromwell himself was
offered the kingship, which he could afford to
refuse because he was already in possession of more
monarchical power than ever the king had had.
With the death of the great man, the nation went
back with relief to its old ways and constitutional
forms; the monarchy was restored in the person
of Charles I's son and heir—to the general
satisfaction. The point is that the Puritan
revolution and the dictatorship of the Army
formed a departure from the normal courses, the
deep ingrained habits of the nation. It is as if a
nation has, by its character and structure, certain
norms which govern its conduct and mould its
institutions. Usually these are so much taken for
granted that they are not in evidence. And in
any case, few people are so sensitive, or so philosophical, as to be conscious of the very elements
in which they live and move. People are never
more aware of these elements, these norms, than
in the moment of departure from them. Hence

the particular self-consciousness, vivacity and value of political thinking in revolutionary periods.

Everyone is aware of how this applies to the French Revolution in the Thermidorian Reaction, when the revolutionary impulse had run its course, made profound changes, perpetrated great excesses, and most normal people were very glad to get back to normal conditions. But let us take a new, and particular instance: the effect of the Revolution upon French foreign policy, the attitude of the French to other peoples.

The outbreak of the Revolution and its first developments—the fall of the Bastille was a universal symbol—raised the hopes of idealists everywhere to a fever-pitch of excitement. Never can there have been such an upsurge of hope, the confident expectation of a new era for mankind, at any historic event. Not only those who were young, and poets, really seem to have thought that it portended a new Heaven and a new Earth. It must have been very delicious to live in that moment, to be borne upon such pinions of enthusiasm. (Such an experience is denied to us, fortunately—for the disillusionment was no less intense.) The mood of the time is expressed in one of the greatest of English poems, *The Prelude:*

Bliss was it in that dawn to be alive,
But to be young was very Heaven! O times,
In which the meagre, stale, forbidding ways

Of custom, law and statute, took at once
The attraction of a country in romance!
When Heaven seemed the most to assert her rights
When most intent on making of herself
A prime enchantress—to assist the work
Which then was going forward in her name!
Not favoured spots alone, but the whole Earth
The beauty wore of promise—that which sets
(As at some moments might not be unfelt
Among the bowers of Paradise itself)
The budding rose above the rose full blown.
What temper at the prospect did not wake
To happiness unthought of?

The Revolution in its first appeal beyond the frontiers of France did bring emancipation and something of the message of universal brotherhood.

But it was not long before more permanent strains in the nature of nations began to assert themselves. It soon became apparent that the appeal to universal brotherhood was an even more effective way of expanding the frontiers of France, of realising the secular objectives of French policy than ever the *ancien régime* had had at its disposal. Soon Belgium and Holland were swallowed up; Switzerland became the Helvetian Republic; Genoa the Ligurian Republic and so on. France was back at her old game, and well on the way to becoming a great military despotism. A European coalition was formed to resist her; Great Britain, a little belatedly, entered the war. Mankind had returned to normal.

The disillusionment on the part of those who had hoped so much was deep and bitter. It has left an undying mark in English literature in the lives and work of Wordsworth, Coleridge, Southey. One can hardly blame them for having hoped too much: they were poets, they were not historians, and they were young. (Older people should have known better what to expect from human beings.) But the experience had a deeply interesting effect on each of them: they all became affected by the historical outlook. Southey became a distinguished historian of the straightforward kind; Coleridge took to metaphysics impregnated with history—from which sprang, among other things, the philosophy of Toryism; Wordsworth turned back for inspiration to Milton and the seventeenth century, and wrote the magnificent patriotic sonnets which are a chief legacy in our literature of the long war with Napoleon.

In French historical literature, the theme of the essential continuity of French policy through the Revolution and under Napoleon with that of the *Ancien Régime* is the subject of Sorel's masterpiece, *L'Europe et la Révolution Française.*

There is the obvious parallel in our own time with the Russian Revolution: the hope, the expectations, the faith; disappointment—the Revolution turning back upon itself, eating its own children; the cynicism, complete disillusionment; the return to normal. Russia has not ceased to be Russia for having been through the October Revolution. It may be called Communist; but Russian society had a strong communal element before, where we are an individualist people. A good deal besides has been continuous too: the absence of political freedom, the authoritarian régime of the Tsars succeeded by that of Stalin, the important part played by the G.P.U. in succession to the old, and less efficient, secret police. The war with Germany brought out all the latent patriotism, the invasion revived all the feeling for the soil of Holy Russia—the themes of 1812 were uppermost—and even brought about a reconciliation between Stalin and the Church. (The association in Russia was always very close; Stalin was educated by the Church.) And we are witnessing, what will be important for the future of Europe, the return to the long-term objectives of Russian policy.

It may be said that these are lessons the application of which is mainly in the past; what of the future? History shows us that there is no such break between the past and the future. While I write this sentence what was future has already become past. All is continuous. And history, without predicting the future, can offer you some useful guide to it. It is probable, for example, that the resumed march of Russia towards her age-long objectives, towards an open Atlantic port, in the Baltic and the Balkans, towards a Mediterranean outlet, in the Middle and Far East, will occupy important pages in what is to come of twentieth-century history.[1] If we do not destroy the nuclei of militant aggression in Germany, or at least neutralise their power to do harm, we shall be faced with another recurrence of the same trouble in a decade or two. What should be the shape of this country's foreign policy in the future? Our best guide is the consistent success of that of the Grand Alliance in the past. In Europe we should construct a system of security in which our interest is at one with that of the great bulk of the whole. Mr. Chamberlain in his ignorance of history thought it possible to have an alliance with Nazi Germany ; had he realised that only a defensive coalition can check an aggressive over-mighty power, we might have avoided the catastrophe that followed 'appeasement.'

With regard to internal politics, it is clear that if we wish to pull our weight in the post-war world we cannot allow our policy to be the prey of a party conflict as from 1921 to 1939: we should be wise to retain the maximum of national unity— as we did throughout the religious conflicts of the Reformation period, and hence our success then, the beginning of our good fortune as a nation. If we are to play our part with success in the more difficult and complex circumstances of the modern

[1] Written in 1944, before the end of the war.

world—we have a promising rôle before us, if we are clever enough to perform it—we cannot afford to allow the conduct of our affairs to fall into the hands of the second-rate men who ran them between the two wars (no wonder we landed ourselves in a second); to choose a Bonar Law, a Baldwin, a Chamberlain, and turn our back upon a Lloyd George and a Churchill. We need Pitts and Cecils, Cannings and Disraelis—and if we can produce them, to use them. In history is our inspiration.

Such are a few of the directives which a common-sense reading of history would suggest for the future.

But that great thinker, Mr. Henry Ford, has told us that 'History is all bunk.' There could not be a more symptomatic expression of the childish superficiality of the modern mechanical mind. It is quite characteristic of the man: when he paid a brief visit to Oxford, nothing of what he saw around him meant anything to that uncultivated—and possibly uncultivable—mind: the only thing he wanted to see was yet another motor-car works. (In that a poor comparison with his English opposite number; for Lord Nuffield's hereditary feeling for—and his generosity to—the University will probably make it the most important centre of advanced medical research in the country.) Mr. Ford really thought in 1927 that he had found the key to the economic problem of our time—with all its maladjustments and strains and conflicts, which had baffled the best intellects of every country—in the simple payment of high wages. In 1929 came the crash of the American boom, and the United States were in for a worse industrial depression than anybody else had had. History, we might say, had caught up with Mr. Ford and had found him to be mostly 'bunk.' As if the United States were any exception to the strains and stresses operating in the modern economic system! Anyone with a knowledge of history, writing at the most plausible period of their boom, should have known that they could not escape the characteristic maladies of capitalism everywhere. In so far as we have now arrived at a better understanding of them, we owe it largely to the historically-minded school of economic thought led by Lord Keynes.

It will be obvious then, that so far from any defeatism about history as a subject of study, I have a blazing confidence in its use. It is a subject that rids you of illusions, one in which you grow up and become adult. The one depressing thought is how little people appear to profit by it. It is rather like what Hegel says—"The one thing one learns from history is that nobody ever learns anything from history." And yet they may learn so much: there is no doubt of that. It offers people an inexhaustible store of vicarious experience upon which they may draw, instead of going through it all over again for themselves in ignorance and (often) suffering.

The price to be paid is a very little trouble for a great deal of pleasure. For in addition to the uses of history, of which I have only elaborated one, there are its pleasures.

In the end, we reflect, man's life is very restricted, confined, in time: a mere three-score and ten years, often not that. If we had only that to go upon we should know very little indeed. The truth is that without the sense of history human life as we know it would be unthinkable; history is as fundamental to our lives as that. It is only through a knowledge of history that our own brief lives—such a short span of experience—become one with the record of the human race; it is only through history that we know anything of that record and can share in it. The life of the individual breaks its barriers and becomes coterminous with humanity. Bound as our lives are to the tyranny of time, it is through what we know of history that we are delivered from our bonds and escape—into time.

Chapter Two

The Pleasures of History

SO far we have been concerned with the utilitarian aspect of the case. But what about the pleasures of history?—and they are many. They may turn out to have a use too: most pleasures have.

Let us begin with what is to me the most obvious, and perhaps the most appealing, pleasure it gives: the way a knowledge of history enriches and fills out our appreciation of the world around us under our eyes. It gives an interest and a meaning to things which perhaps we should not have noticed before, not only villages and towns and buildings, a church, an old house, a bridge, but even the landscape itself.

Half a mile away from my home in Cornwall there is a field, just above the farm of Castle Gotha right on the cliffs, which I had crossed for years before I realised what it was. The name 'Castle Gotha' ought to have aroused my suspicions, given me a clue. You go through the kissing-gates on the road to Trenarren and find yourself in a big enclosure with a magnificent view of the bay and all the inland country to the china-clay uplands. When you pass out through the kissing-gates at the other side, you find yourself in a little lane: it is the remains of the dyke of a prehistoric camp with the broad vallum rising on your left and running away in a semicircle. Under your feet as you go, you feel the hard track that crosses the field to the headland, where there is a well-marked prehistoric cliff-fortification. In the field on the other side of my house is a great longstone, one of the finest monoliths in Cornwall, which still has its aura of superstition and fear among the local people of these parts. ("As children we never played in that field," a woman once told me; "they do say that a man was hanged there once—oh, hundreds of years ago.") Further along in the depression where the road goes down to Charlestown there was a number of barrows, demolished when the road was made to the little port.

You begin to see a picture of the life of the primitive folk around this bay in prehistoric times, as it was, say, from 1000 B.C. to 500 A.D.: the camp at Castle Gotha which was their 'town,' their stronghold; the cliff-camp to which they could retire when danger was greatest—it is a very narrow isthmus across the headland, defended by two considerable vallums or ramparts, and there is a spring of water in the cliff. There is the monolith facing east and west—a most impressive figure it makes in the setting sun—that was the centre of their religious rites, almost certainly involving human sacrifice; there were the barrows where they buried their great dead, the chiefs of the tribe.

I am no pre-historian, nor an archæologist; but when I put together the picture of these remains from prehistoric times, and read a little about those times in Gordon Childe's *Prehistoric Communities of the British Isles*, I confess that the whole thing came alive for me: the life lived around the bay gained a whole dimension: one could see it, the continuous life of those earlier folk, the "Mediterranean men, my ancestors," going right back to the dim savage shades of unrecorded antiquity.

How much more fascinating—at least to me— are the periods of which we have record.

From my study window I look straight out across the blue waves and white horses of the bay to the headlands on either side of the entrance to Fowey harbour. And I remember the medieval and Elizabethan appearance of that delightful town with all its history. The earlier dedication of the church, to St. Finbarrus of Cork, tells us of the town's important trade with Ireland in the Middle Ages: Irish merchants formed a considerable contingent of the early settlers who made the town.

In the Middle Ages Fowey was much the most important of Cornish ports: under its leadership they sent forty-seven ships, a larger contribution than any other save London's, to the armada with which Edward III besieged Calais

in 1347. In the church, in the Treffry chapel,
are the achievements of John Treffry who fought
under the Black Prince at Poictiers and took the
French royal standard. That chapel is full of
their memorials, of the brothers Sir John, William
and Thomas, who were very well known to
Henry VIII and Cromwell, and took an active
part on the side of the Reformation in Cornwall.
Above the church towers their fine house of
Place, which an earlier Treffry lady of the
fifteenth century had defended heroically against
the French when they burnt the town. That was
a reprisal for the depredations of John Mixtow
and the merry men of Fowey upon French ships
in the Channel—you may read about it in C. L.
Kingsford's sedate *Prejudice and Promise in the
Fifteenth Century*. When I walk through those
vivacious, angular, cramped streets I always
think as I look up at the windows of Place—that
decorated stone front overlooking all the town—
of another episode in English history: of Philip II's
chests of gold, intended for the payment of Alva's
troops in the Netherlands in 1569, which were
'interned' for the Queen at Saltash and Fowey, and
those very same chests reposing in Mr. Treffry's
cellars until fetched up to the Tower of London.
For want of that cash, Alva's troops mutinied—
which gave a breathing-space to the Nether-
landers fighting for their liberty; and it was a very
important turning-point in the relations between
England and Spain.

34

On the other side of the lime-walk from the church is the Ship Inn—the old house of the Rashleighs, not far from the quay where they did business so profitably in the days of Elizabeth. Upstairs you may still see the black oak-panelled best room of John Rashleigh and his wife Alice, with a fine carved mantelpiece supported by caryatids—the impulse of the Italian Renaissance reaching this remote West-country spot; the date, 1570. They both of them lie quiet enough now in the church across the way; Alice under her chaste brass beneath the pulpit, her husband in full Elizabethan black gown and white ruff upon his painted tomb. They owned a famous little ship, the *Francis* of Fowey, which made a fortune for them as a privateer in those disturbed days in the Channel and the Bay of Biscay. Their son sailed her up to Plymouth to fight under Drake against the Armada in 1588. The next generation bought land; left Fowey and commerce for the lovely Gribbin peninsula, where they built their home at Menabilly—still looking out to sea. A generation later the Civil War descended upon them there; and precisely three hundred years ago this very summer in which I write, the Parliamentarian army under Essex was cooped up in that peninsula by the Royalist army under the King and forced to surrender—but not before they had eaten all Mr. Rashleigh's cattle and livestock, 10,000 sheep (so he claimed). From these fields—then open downs—you must have been able to see all the soldiery swarming over that narrow neck of land.

And so one could go on—but I am not writing a history of Fowey. (I wish someone would!) I am merely showing you how the whole landscape comes alive when you know the history that lies behind it. Nor is it only martial events like sieges and battles, civil wars and the burning of towns, that light it up. There is all the romance and pathos of industry, the mines that were once hives sounding with the activity of hundreds of men, now all closed down, ruined shells of engine-houses, the refuse dumps once more carpeted with green.

> The places that are empty now
> Were once so full of vivid life.

In the near foreground upon the cliffs stands the shell of Appletree mine; the workings went far out under the bay. To the left, where now Campdowns spreads its garment of gorse and withies and ash, was a rich mining district with a number of mines. They all had to close down in the eighteen seventies and eighties, and hundreds of men left home to work the mines in South Africa, Montana, Michigan, Australia. Quite near across the cornfield is Charlestown Foundry, the oldest foundry in Cornwall to be working continuously to this day. It must be a hundred and fifty years old—and it has done its part in this war, turning out—well, I won't say what. But all this—the

nineteenth-century mining development of Cornwall, the pathetic emigration of thousands of
Cornish miners all over the world (you will come
across one of them portrayed in Stevenson's
Across the Plains)—it is all a part of the great story
of the Industrial Revolution which looms so
formidably in the text-books under that name.
(Read about it in C. R. Fay's *English Economic
History from 1760* and you will find it fascinating.)

If this is only one tithe of what comes to mind
from looking out of a window in Cornwall, upon a
small and not particularly significant part of the
English scene, you can imagine what richness,
what delights there are in walking the streets of a
town like Oxford, or Bristol, or York, or Carlisle,
or Edinburgh, or London. I cannot begin to give
you an idea of what it is like to live in a place like
Oxford, there are so many layers of memories and
associations, there is no end to the pleasure of
exploring them. Not that I have set out deliber-
ately to explore them—for I have made Cornwall
my chosen field of investigation; it is just that
they come to mind and fill every moment with
interest and fascination. When I go down into
the quadrangle I think of Froude, wonderful
writer that he was, turning in at the gate of All
Souls from the traffic of the High and in the
quietness meditating upon the Oxford of thirty
years before, the Oxford of Newman and the
Tractarians. From my room I can always see
the spire of Newman's St. Mary's, the University

37

church, which has those other memories, Cranmer's last withdrawal of his recantation on the way to the stake, Amy Robsart's burial in the chancel. Or if I walk in the Meadows there is the Civil War that conjures up scenes in my mind: poor young Colonel Windebank being shot against the city wall that is the boundary of Merton College—a romantic story, that; Merton itself the palace of Henrietta Maria, the King housed in Christ Church: they made a door through the wall that the two might visit each other privately. And often on my pedestrian way to the station, bent prosaically upon catching a train, I catch sight of the Norman tower of the Castle; and as often as not my mind goes back to Geoffrey of Monmouth, who was a canon of the chapel there in the twelfth century, and wrote his work on the *Histories of the Kings of Britain* in those remote far-away days. Never was there a book that had a more prodigious influence upon the literatures of Europe, save only the Bible; for from it came the incredible flowering of the Arthurian legend in all the languages and arts of Western Europe, in French, Italian, German, English, Spanish. Think only in our own language of Malory and Spenser, of Tennyson, Arnold, Swinburne and Hardy, who all go back to that twelfth-century book written somewhere down that forgotten road. (But it shall not be forgotten by me: better to miss any number of trains than forget that!)

You may say that Oxford is a very special case, as in a way it is. Living there as a boy was an inspiration to one great English historian, J. R. Green: he was born there, went to Magdalen College School, grew up in its streets, loving every nook and cranny of the place, and before he ceased to be an undergraduate had written the first of his famous essays, " Oxford in the Last Century." It came out as a series of articles in the local paper, the *Oxford Chronicle*. But already it is not a far cry to his wonderful *Short History of the English People*: such masterpieces have such beginnings.

My point is that every old town is a special case. Many of them have beauty—alas, much damaged and crippled not merely by the Teutonic barbarian but by our own barbarians who know nothing either of history or beauty, who, in fact, being uneducated in the full sense of the word, know nothing, see nothing, understand nothing, appreciate nothing, and whose lives are certainly brutish, if they are unfortunately neither solitary nor short. These old towns all have their own character and interest. Think of Norwich, full of churches and the feeling of being a great centre still of medieval trade; of Bristol with its finger on the pulses of the sea and all those voyages going out of the port to America, and the monuments of the merchants in the city churches. Or there is Carlisle, with its sombre sense of a border fortress town, the fine West Walks overlooking the flats, the Castle looking out over the Debatable Lands to Scotland; one thinks of Mary Queen of Scots viewing from the ramparts the football match between her retinue and the garrison. Or York, with its magnificent sense of space and of being a capital. How many kings have entered the city in triumph or in defeat; there is the tragic figure of the great Lord President of the North, Strafford, that haunts the splendid house that once was the abbot's of St. Mary's; or a more endearing shade, the whimsical, fantastic man of genius, Laurence Sterne, finding it difficult to stand up to his formidable uncle, treasurer of the Minster. (You get an exquisite feeling for the memories of the city in one of the most nostalgic autobiographies of our time, Margaret Mann Phillips' *Within the City Wall*.) Or there is Edinburgh, most striking and perhaps the most exciting town in these islands, stretched out along that bitter spine of rock between the Castle and Holyrood—each with its dramatic stories, the little room in the palace where the Scottish lords hacked Rizzio to death in the presence of their Queen; the more genial shadow on the blind of the quick pen racing across the pages, the unknown 'author of *Waverley*.' Or there is London. It is difficult for us English people to see London from the outside or grasp its character. We take it so much for granted—far too much for granted: it is the terminus of all our journeys, a world, a fate: there is something inevitable about it. But a distinguished Dane, Rasmussen, who has written a very good book on it, says—what we cannot tell—that it has a *stronger* character of its own than any other town in the world.

When you come to great towns like London, or Paris, or Vienna, or Rome—or Edinburgh, Antwerp, Florence, Madrid—you reach the plane of historic events on an international scale. Their memories are inexhaustible, of the greatest events and men.

I have taken you from history in the immediate vicinity to history played on the largest stage of national and international affairs. Let us return to the parish. For here there is not only the pleasure awaiting you when you begin to open your eyes and store your mind, but the pleasure you can pursue across country with much less trouble and expense than following the hounds.

Walking is the favourite sport of 'the good and the wise.' This is not the place to sing its praises in and for itself; that has been done by more siren voices than mine, by Leslie Stephen and Meredith, by R. L. Stevenson and G. M. Trevelyan, best of all by Hazlitt. I want to make a point that is not made by any of them, not even by Trevelyan, oddly enough: perhaps it classes me among the heterodox, not to say heretical, walkers. Walking is the way to see the country: there is no other way, certainly not going by motor-car. But what a great addition it is to the pleasure of walking to have some interesting object in view: to saunter through an old village, linger in the church over the monuments and things of beauty, eat your sandwiches by a ford that had its part in the Wars of the Roses, trespass as far as you can through the park to get a good view of the old mansion, still Tudor in its main lines, though you mark with interest the seventeenth- and eighteenth-century additions—calling up in the mind the continuous life of the family there through all the changes of the Henries, Edwards, Elizabeth, the Georges. Later in the afternoon you rest at a spot where you can look down upon the outlines of a Roman villa in the valley below, or you step aside to view a stone circle—perhaps the Rollright stones in the northern Cotswolds which Shakespeare must often have looked at with that curious observant eye. You may, if you are good and it is not war-time, have tea in an old inn, in the porch of which (if it is Devon) the charming Cavalier poet Sidney Godolphin died, or where (if it is Oxford-shire) the great John Hampden lingered his last days.

The country is infinitely rich in memories, and old buildings, country houses or yeoman's farm, barn or bridge or byre. And every parish has its church, usually an old one, with its memorials left behind by the tides and currents of life that have flowed through it. Any walk you choose to take can have a fascination for a cultivated mind. One would not be uncultivated for anything. For that way lies infinite boredom and dreariness of

THE PLEASURES OF HISTORY

spirit. The truest thing—and the most useful—
that ever Dean Inge said was that "the true
intellectual is never bored." And what a strength
that is when you come to think of it. A friend
of mine, the Cornish antiquary and historian,
Charles Henderson, had the habit from his schooldays of walking or taking bus or train to some
particular parish and then settling down upon it
for the day, traversing it, following its boundaries,
looking up everything of interest in it, camp
or stone-circle, holy-well or chapel, villages and
farms. Often it meant several visits, returning to
the same parish. It was that that filled out and
made real and concrete his remarkable knowledge
of documents and deeds relating to the past. In
this way he came to know not only every parish
and church in Cornwall, but almost every farm
and field. This is the way that historians are
made. It could not be better put than by R. H.
Tawney when he tells us that what economic
history needs at present is not more documents but
a pair of sturdy boots.

This advice is for current historians, all too
many of whom need it or they would be more alive
and readable than they are. But the pleasure and
fun of it are for all to enjoy.

Then there is reading. Perhaps I should have
dealt with this first, since most people think of
history in terms of books to read. But I wanted to
drive home that the things we see around us, a town
or village, a church, a harbour or bit of wall, even

a field or a stretch of landscape, are all documents for history as much as a charter or land-book, a title-deed, a letter or a will. Very often the two relate to each other, the land to the title-deed, the house and its furnishings to the will, the landscape to the letter. They illuminate each other. The point about the written evidences is that they are usually more precise; of their nature they define what is in question; often they will give you the date, or the place of the event in the sequence of the story.

There is a famous and too-much discussed dictum of Croce's, "All history is contemporary history." I do not think there is more in it than this, that we know the past only through the evidences that survive, directly or indirectly, into the present and are in our minds now, as with any other knowledge. Not a particularly valuable thought. Of course there is more implied in it than that, and some of what is implied is very debatable: we may be able to turn to it later. But this approach to history is sound in so far as it comes to this, in common-sense terms: that the past is not something dead, shut away like a series of damp catacombs, which you enter by a difficult and uncongenial mode of ingress (in other words, an examination-course on unappetising text-books)—it is alive and about you. History is about life and has the appeal of life itself; the feeling for history is a nostalgia for life, subtly transmuted. That is the answer to the question

of one of the most academic—and at the same time
poetic—of present-day historians, F. M. Powicke:
"Shepherds have kept their sheep in all ages:
why am I stirred so deeply because I can trace the
very sheep-walks of the monks of Furness? Why
is there a remote, yet strangely familiar, music
about the names of places—Beverley, Gains-
borough, Thrapston, Tewkesbury—a music in
which it is impossible to distinguish the call of
authentic English speech from the echoes of a
hundred insistent associations? . . . It is the
sense of the past that comes to us from the Middle
Ages as it came to the young American in Henry
James's story, as he wandered about his eighteenth-
century house in London—'the sense of a conscious past, recognizing no less than recognizable.'
The place was a museum, 'but a museum of held
reverberations.' So long as we are conscious of
these 'held reverberations,' history will continue to
entice us. So long as their mystery endures, and
it will always endure, the past will continue to
escape us."

That opens up another and subtler question,
which we shall return to.

Because history is vibrant with life, pulsates
with it—Carlyle said that it was the essence of
innumerable biographies—reading biographies is
a very good way of beginning to read history.
Perhaps it is the best of all for beginners. Everybody is interested in personality; everybody loves
a story—or he is a very dull dog who does not.

And that makes me very much in favour of the biographical approach, especially with children, in teaching history in schools. Everybody knows, or should know, that the important thing is to arouse their interest. It applies not only to children but to all of us. It is merely sound psychology that we find it infinitely easier to pick up knowledge that interests us than what doesn't interest us. (I cannot drive a car, for instance, because I am not the least bit interested in anything mechanical: I suffer from what the Church calls a state of invincible ignorance on the subject.) But the life of a human being, particularly an exciting one, fascinates me; and the great figures of history have all had exciting lives. For me there is no end to the interest in the extraordinary personalities of people like Queen Elizabeth, Cromwell, Nelson, Swift, William the Silent, Richelieu, Peter the Great, the Empress Catherine, Lenin, Lloyd George, Clemenceau, Winston Churchill.

There is one obvious danger in reading history from biographies: you may get a one-sided view of the subject. The remedy for this is to read the lives of men on both sides. As Trevelyan says: "The lives of rival statesmen, warriors and thinkers, provided they are good books, are often the quickest route to the several points of view that composed the life of an epoch. *Ceteris paribus*, a single biography is more likely to mislead than a history of the period, but several biographies are often more deeply instructive than a single history."

I have only scratched the surface of the interest in human personality that is excited, and satisfied, by historical biography. In truth, in its full depth and in the round, the appeal is the same as that of characters in a novel, of characters in a great novel. There is the conflict of characters, the mutual likes and dislikes, the loves and hatreds; the conflicts within one person, the irrationalities, the divided loyalties; there is the subtle complexity of motive; the strange patterns that our lives fall into, the drama and tragedy of so many of them upon the public scene. The people in Tolstoy's *War and Peace* have the same appeal as that of the actual people in history. In historical writing there is always and at every point the limitation of truth; but that is an advantage as much as a limitation. Tolstoy was not confined to telling the truth about Napoleon; the result is that we get a very unfair and biased account of him. Napoleon was a far more wonderful man—in spite of his obvious defects— than Tolstoy gives us any idea of. On the other hand, if we take a character like Turgeniev's Bazarov (in *Fathers and Children*), he is just like a portrait out of Herzen's *Memoirs*, just as authentic and convincing.

Then there is the pleasure, and the importance, of the story in itself. It is here, perhaps, that contemporary historians are weakest. They are

not entirely to be blamed for it; for it is partly due
to the enormous increase in the amount of subject-
matter—economic, social, archæological, what
not—to be subsumed in a modern history. The
extension of the range of history is all to the good;
and as and when the absorption of the new
material advances, the ability of contemporary
historians to cope with it improves, one may expect the art of narrative to return to its central
position in historical writing. For after all, the
very word 'history,' the fact that it is cognate with
'story,' shows you that narrative is the backbone
of history.

Its appeal, and the pleasure of it, are elemental.
It is as primitive and fundamental in a society as
that of the epic, of the *Iliad* and *Odyssey*, or of the
Icelandic sagas. It is the *story* that holds our
attention in childhood, as in the childhood of
peoples. The concern with truth, the delimita-
tion of fact from fiction—in short, the development of historical writing—is a later, more sophisticated stage. Thucydides is many centuries
later than Homer; Gibbon centuries later than
Chaucer. All the same it is essentially the story
in both Thucydides and Gibbon that grips the
mind: it marches on remorselessly like a tragedy
to its inevitable end, like Meredith's

"army of unalterable law,"

or like the sea across the bay under my eyes as I
write.

But was it inevitable, unalterable? Ah, there begin the subtle and exciting *intellectual* issues of history. For the present we will confine ourselves to the remark that the appeal of the story is like that of *Gulliver's Travels*, one that grows with you as you grow in mind, ripens with your own experience of life, deepens and comes to have much more meaning for you as you achieve maturity. In childhood it may have the same appeal as a fairy-story or a tale of adventure; in later life it may come to have a philosophical meaning for you. Therein lies a large part of the satisfaction in historical study: it is a study that grows with you: a subject that was capable of interesting you as a child does not fail to reward you, but has an even deeper interest for the grown man.

Nearly all the great historians—though not every one of them—have been masters of narration. As we have seen, it was easier for them than for us with the vast masses of material, and of such different kinds, for us to absorb into our books. All the same, it was never absolutely easy: it demanded art, craftsmanship, long labour. Gibbon took years learning to write—and with what results! In our time when there are so many people writing who are not artists, and so many writing history who take far more trouble searching for new material than composing what they find, nothing like enough attention is paid to composition, arrangement, style. That makes inferior writers more difficult to read. " But easy writing's vile hard reading," said Sheridan. No such difficulty with Macaulay, who took infinite pains with his writing. "In arrangement," Trevelyan says, "that is to say in the planning of the book, in the way subject leads on to subject and paragraph to paragraph, Macaulay's *History* has no equal and ought to be carefully studied by everyone who intends to write a narrative history."

Hence it is that historians are among the great writers of most ages which have achieved maturity and sophistication—for reflection upon the past is a sign of maturity, and there is something sophisticated in the desire to tell only the truth, that essential and self-willed limitation upon the historian. Thucydides was among the very greatest of Greek writers in antiquity, and Herodotus, the founder of a different tradition, the father of both social history and anthropology, comes but little behind him. Livy and Tacitus are among the great Roman writers, as Commines and Froissart are among those of medieval France, or Machiavelli and Guicciardini of Renaissance Italy. Though we have no Shakespeare or Milton among English historians, it is not altogether inappropriate to compare Clarendon, who stands at the head of the English tradition of historical writing, to Milton. There is the same magnificent architectonic sense, the marshalling of experience, the same deep undercurrent of emotion. And though *Paradise Lost* is great poetry, there is perhaps more romantic feeling in Clarendon. Gibbon and Hume are among the very greatest writers of their age; Carlyle, Macaulay, Froude of theirs. And lesser historians even, J. R. Green, Creighton, Seeley, Acton, are distinguished men of letters. All these historians, and many more, offer you the delights of literature. On a recent long train-journey, from Cornwall to London, I took a volume of Gibbon and *Bleak House* with me. Though I have a very high admiration for *Bleak House* as a novel, I found Gibbon more enthralling as well as more amusing.

There is another aspect of this question of the relations between history and literature. Historians not only contribute directly to literature, but a knowledge of history enters in varying degrees into the appreciation of literature. Perhaps it enters least into the appreciation of pure poetry or drama, and most into that of political literature where the subject-matter is bound up with history. Because the English have long been a politically conscious and politically competent people—and because they are an infinitely creative people—they have a quick and varied political literature, from Sir Thomas More and Tyndale to Bacon and Hooker and Ralegh; Milton and Hobbes and Locke; Swift and Burke; Hazlitt, Carlyle, John Stuart Mill. In much of what these men wrote it is essential to know some history to know what they are talking about, what are the issues being discussed.

It is not only in this realm of literature that a knowledge of history is helpful or even indispensable, it may be with regard to novels—the novels of Scott and Disraeli, for example, or for that matter of Stendhal and Balzac, or some of the novels of Flaubert, Tolstoy, Turgeniev. Nor does it end here. It may be of the greatest value in enabling you to understand, and derive a much fuller pleasure from, the drama—the plays of Shakespeare, or of the Restoration theatre, of Dryden and Congreve, Goldsmith and Sheridan. The same holds good of a great deal of poetry, of Milton and Dryden, Wordsworth, Scott and Byron. *The Prelude* is possibly the greatest work of literature to owe its impulse to the French Revolution, and it is not properly understandable without knowing something of Wordsworth's relation to that universal event. But even works of a more remote, a more purely poetic character, like Spenser's *Faerie Queene*, or Tennyson's *Idylls of the King*, are illuminated for us, and our pleasure heightened, by a knowledge of the history that has gone into them and the contemporary background which they in part express. And we may savour something of the latter even in the purest lyric poetry—say Christina Rossetti's *Goblin Market*. Of course the æsthetic reaction to a work of art comes first in the case of literature—that should go without saying; but the historic appreciation in no way conflicts with it: it complements it and fills it out.

Reading history, then, opens out fresh fields,

illimitable beckoning horizons to the imagination. The pleasure of it, as Macaulay says, " is analogous, in many respects, to that produced by foreign travel. The student, like the tourist, is transported into a new state of society. He sees new fashions. He hears new modes of expression. His mind is enlarged by contemplating the wide diversities of laws, of morals and of manners. But men may travel far, and return with minds so contracted as if they had never stirred from their own market town." And so Macaulay makes his plan for sinking shafts deep into society and writing the whole life, as far as possible, of a people, not resting content with a lifeless skeleton of the names and dates of battles and genealogies of royal houses. "He who would understand these rightly must not confine his observations to palaces and solemn days. He must see ordinary men as they appear in their ordinary business and in their ordinary pleasures. He must mingle in the crowds of the exchange and the coffee-house. He must obtain admittance to the convivial table and the domestic hearth. He must bear with vulgar expressions. He must not shrink from exploring even the retreats of misery. He who wishes to understand the condition of mankind in former ages must proceed on the same principle." Such was Macaulay's programme in the brilliant essay on history which he wrote as a young man for the *Edinburgh Review*. In maturity he carried out his precepts in the famous third chapter of his *History*, on the state of society in the age, which helped to account for the extraordinary enthusiasm with which the book was received. Macaulay himself modestly declared, "I shall not be satisfied unless I produce something which shall for a few days supersede the last fashionable novel on the tables of young ladies." He succeeded in producing a book that has held the attention of the English-speaking world undiminished for the last century.

In the end, then, we see history as a compound of fact and imagination, of the imagination picturing the facts, lapping round them, like the sea round the rocks upon the coast. The province of the intellect is to interpret the facts, reduce them to order, extract their significance. (We shall come to that later.) But, as Trevelyan says, "at bottom the appeal of history is imaginative. Our imagination craves to behold our ancestors as they really were, going about their daily business and their daily pleasure. . . . It is the detailed study of history that makes us feel that the past was as real as the present. . . . It is only by study that we can see our fore-runners remote and recent, in their habits as they lived, intent each on the business of a long-vanished day, riding out to do homage or to poll a vote; to seize a neighbour's manor house and carry off his ward, or to leave cards on ladies in crinolines. . . . Truth is the criterion of historical study; but its impelling motive is poetic."

54

All the great historians have felt this; though not all of them have been equally able—or perhaps even wished—to express it. But the fact is that the experience at the heart of our feeling for history is a great deal closer to poetry than is generally realised; in truth, I think it is in essence the same. The moment of illumination which Wordsworth expressed in "Tintern Abbey," in the ode on "Intimations of Immortality," and again and again in *The Prelude*, is not essentially different from the moment of evocation and perception at the core of the historian's experience. The historians have given expression to it, but I know that many people who are not historians share it and know what I mean. Froude has captured it in a wonderful and justly famous passage of his *History*:

"For, indeed, a change was coming upon the world, the meaning and direction of which even still is hidden from us, a change from era to era. The paths trodden by the footsteps of ages were broken up; old things were passing away, and the faith and the life of ten centuries were dissolving like a dream. Chivalry was dying; the abbey and the castle were soon together to crumble into ruins; and all the forms, desires, beliefs, convictions of the old world were passing away, never to return. A new continent had risen up beyond the western sea. The floor of heaven, inlaid with stars, had sunk back into an infinite abyss of immeasurable space; and the firm earth itself, unfixed from its foundations, was seen to be but a small atom in the awful vastness of the universe. In the fabric of habit in which they had so laboriously built for themselves, mankind were to remain no longer.

"And now it is all gone—like an unsubstantial pageant faded; and between us and the old English there lies a gulf of mystery which the prose of the historian will never adequately bridge. They cannot come to us, and our imagination can but feebly penetrate to them. Only among the aisles of our cathedrals, only as we gaze upon their silent figures sleeping on their tombs, some faint conceptions float before us of what these men were when they were alive; and perhaps in the sound of church bells, that peculiar creation of medieval age, which falls upon the ear like the echo of a vanished world."

But at any moment the experience may take us unawares, when something recalls the past: not necessarily the conscious prose of the great historian; it may be a fifteenth-century merchant of the Staple away at Calais, writing to his girl-bride in Oxfordshire:

"Be a good eater of your meat alway, that ye may wax and grow fat to be a woman . . . and greet well my horse and pray him to give you four of his years to help you withal. And I will at my coming home give him four of my years and four horse-loaves to make amends. Tell him that I prayed him so. . . . And Almighty Jesu make you a good woman and send you alway many good years and long to live in health and virtue to his pleasure. Written at Calais the first of June, when every man was gone to his dinner, and the clock smote noon and all our household cried after me and bade me come down. 'Come down to dinner at once!' And what answer I gave to them ye know of old."

One's heart stands still: it is one of those moments when time falls away from us: our feeling for that man who has been dead for centuries is the feeling for ourselves, the sense of our own life slipping away even as his.

The love of history is, then, an expression—not the less beautiful, but the more poignant, for being transmuted, indirect—of the love of life.

Chapter Three

What History is About

NOW perhaps for a dull chapter of definitions. There are two ways of thinking of history. There is, first, history regarded as a way of looking at other things, really the temporal aspect of anything, from the universe to this nib with which I am writing. Everything has its history. There is the history of the universe, if only we knew it—and we know something of it, if we do not know much. Nor is the contrast so great, when you come to think of it, between the universe and this pen-nib. A mere pen-nib has quite a considerable history. There is, to begin with, what has been written with it, and that might be something quite important. After all it was probably only one quill-pen or a couple that wrote *Hamlet*. Whatever has been written with the pen-nib is part of its history. In addition to that there is the history of its manufacture: this particular nib is a 'Relief' nib, No. 314, made by R. Esterbrook and Co. in England, who supply the Midland Bank with pen-nibs, from whom I got it—a gift, I may say. But behind this nib there is the whole process of manufacture; I do not know the processes, but you could learn them and you would find that you had quite an introduction to the history of the Industrial Revolution. Beyond that there are the various metals that have gone into the making of the nib: I do not know what they are, iron and tin and copper I suppose, nor do I know where they come from: the iron may have come from Sweden, the copper from Spain, the tin from Malaya. Anyhow, you see that the history of a mere pen-nib involves you in the processes of industry, in a knowledge of geography and of geology, and there is no knowing what else may be relevant, in greater or lesser degree. In fact a pen-nib implies the universe, and the history of it implies *its* history.

We may regard this way of looking at it— history as the time-aspect of all things: a pen-nib, the universe, the field before me as I write, a person (perhaps you who are reading me now), an institution—the church you belong to, or this country to which we both belong—as a relative conception of history.

There is, secondly, what we may call a substantive conception of history, what we usually mean by it, history proper as a subject of study in itself.

What is history, as a subject in itself, about then?

Sir Charles Firth gives us something to begin on: "History is not easy to define; but to me it seems the record of the life of societies of men, of the changes which those societies have gone

59

through, of the ideas which have determined the actions of those societies, and of the material conditions which have helped or hindered their development."

That seems to me an excellent working definition, not necessarily exhaustive, but at any rate central to the subject. Notice that it is much wider than you might expect from an old-fashioned nineteenth-century historian, what the Marxists call a *bourgeois* historian. Firth was indeed an academic historian of the purest water. He made no concessions whatever to the reader, or to anybody else. He had the strictest and most exacting standards of scholarship; he had a searching critical sense, the keenest edge to his intellect. This, added to a certain defect in his emotional nature, a North-country grittiness of mind, inhibited him as a writer. He was a devotee of the impersonal in history—as if you can cease being yourself, however impersonal you may try to be! The result was that he was the finest example of the historical scholar of his time, rather than the finest historian. He was in truth an historians' historian, in the way that some poets, like Spenser for example, are peculiarly the choice of their fellows, or Flaubert a novelists' novelist. Firth exemplified in himself his own catholic principle of scholarship: of his own period, the seventeenth century, no one has ever known more. He knew more than Macaulay; and this extraordinary detailed knowledge extended forward to include a great deal of the eighteenth century and backward to include much of the sixteenth. He set himself to know all that there was to be known about his period, not only the documents in print and in manuscript, but the literature.

My point is that though Firth was the type of the academic historian, in truth he was altogether more catholic and comprehensive than Marxist writers who criticise the type without being able to provide a better example. His own writings covered many aspects of his period; he contributed not to one only but to several fields of history. The biggest of his books, his continuation of Gardiner's history, *The Last Years of the Protectorate*, belongs to political history. *The House of Lords during the Civil War* is an important contribution to constitutional history. His book *Cromwell's Army* is a standard work in military history, his life of Oliver Cromwell the most authoritative biography. There are many essays, studies and editions of works, which are contributions not only to the history of literature but to social history. And though he did not write specifically on economic history, an essay like his "London in the Civil War" attests his appreciation of the importance of the economic factor.

Firth's predecessor at Oxford, York Powell, had a similarly wide conception of what history should be, even if he did not carry it out in his own exiguous writing. "It deals with the condition of masses of mankind living in a social state. It seeks to discover the laws that govern these conditions and bring about changes we call Progress and Decay, and Development and Degeneracy—to understand the processes that gradually or suddenly make up or break up those political and economic agglomerations we call States—to find out the circumstances affecting the various tendencies that show their power at different times."

These wide and sympathetic views were developed no doubt in conscious reaction to the limitation of history to political history. The arch-apostle of this view was Seeley, who was in the habit of insisting to his pupils that "the history of the Staffordshire Potteries was *not* history." He was only interested really in the life of the state, and the conflicts of power between states: he was much influenced by German models. Not being a brilliant writer himself, he did not hold with history as literature. Trevelyan enters a gentle protest at having been solemnly instructed as an undergraduate at Cambridge "by the author of *Ecce Homo* that Macaulay and Carlyle did not know what they were writing about, and that 'literary history' was a thing of naught." The reaction in Trevelyan's case has done nothing but good.

I agree with Firth and York Powell—and for that matter with the Marxists—that history is essentially the record of the life of men in societies in their geographical and physical environment. Their social and cultural environment arises from the interaction of the one with the other, the society and its geographical conditions. You may say that the process is even a dialectical one—though I should prefer not to use such words; it is certainly a dynamic one.

That gives you the groundwork of history; it is not the background: it is the story itself: the story of human society, or the stories of human societies. And it is upon that groundwork that all the variety and detail of history arises. The individual is a social product: the child of given parents in a certain condition of life, a member of a particular family with marked characteristics; he belongs to a particular class of society, is moulded and made by school and friends and church and university. But the converse is also true: society is made up of individuals, and history is made up of millions of particular events and instances. Some schools of thought emphasise the one, other schools emphasise the other. To my mind there is no real conflict between the mass and the individual in the proper understanding of history. They are complementary to each other. The mass is more important in determining the long-term course of events; understanding the mass-movements of society is more important to *understanding* history. The individual is more important in the realm of values; it is his standards that evaluate those movements. It is the life of the individual that is the ultimate thing in human experience. We may say that the importance of the one is intellectual and scientific, of the other spiritual and æsthetic. And it depends on what angle you are tackling the subject from, which approach is more appropriate and should be given more prominence.

We have an ideal, then, of history as the history of society *as a whole*. Neither Firth nor York Powell carried out his precept; the latter never tried to. One can well understand why—because of the innate difficulty of the task. I understand those difficulties, having attempted an example of such a total history in my *Tudor Cornwall*. If you are going to portray a whole society in all its aspects, its geographical environment, its economic foundation, the land system and its industries, the governmental and administrative system, the social structure, the political events, the social, religious and cultural life—it is probable that it can only be done at all fully for a small society and in miniature. If the scale becomes much enlarged it becomes almost impossible to do it and to retain the concrete, pictorial treatment; the work may have to become a work of synthesis and lose vivid individuality. Yet the impulse towards this kind of total history —giving an account of a society in all its aspects— is unmistakable in contemporary writing. The idea behind the new Oxford History of England reflects it, though a series of text-books can hardly exemplify it. The first volume of Halévy's *History of the English People in the Nineteenth Century*, devoted to describing the condition of England in 1815, affords a better example with a larger canvas. With Trevelyan's *England in the Age of Queen Anne* it has produced a masterpiece.

Having declared my sympathy with the movement for total history, I may perhaps be allowed to return to the case of political history. Since we agree that it is the life of the whole society that we are portraying, with its movements, its conflicts, its *bêtises* and its achievements, its groups and individual figures, it is clear that politics has a central place; for it is upon the plane of politics that all these things are projected and expressed. Politics consists of the public behaviour of men in the mass; it is the society's sphere of action. It is of central importance in the life of a society. And similarly political history must always be the backbone of history. The greatest histories— Thucydides, Gibbon, Macaulay—are all obviously and necessarily political histories. In the contemporary reaction against a too narrow, political interpretation there is some danger of this being forgotten. That is why I welcome with complete agreement these words of G. N. Clark: "I will even venture to say that we ought still to treat the life of each community in each period as a whole.

Many historians are indeed now dissatisfied with the old way of taking political and constitutional history as the central thread through the diversity. Economic history has vindicated its right to a high place; social history puts forward a strong claim. But it is in public institutions that men express their will to control events, and therefore it seems to me that historians will go wrong if they try to resolve political and constitutional history into other elements, just as our practical men will go wrong if they follow the current fashion of treating 'cultural' interests and activities as if they could be altogether separated from the affairs of states. The history of institutions must be in some sense central."

This last sentence gives us a clue to some further definitions. Political and constitutional history are very close together: political history is the record of the public events in the life of the society, constitutional history gives you the story of its institutions, the political and administrative framework that keeps the society together and enables it to work. Some people make a further distinction between constitutional and administrative history, but you need not trouble to remember it, for they are indeed the same thing. It happens that in the nineteenth century, owing to the great political changes that were taking place, an immense stimulus was given to the study of constitutional history. Two of our greatest historians were specialists in this field: Stubbs, who wrote a great *Constitutional History of England*, and Maitland. The generation after them, led by Tout, tended to concentrate on the lesser institutions, filling up the gaps and reinterpreting some of the evidence. So that one may say without unfairness, I think, that administrative history is a lesser, and apt to be a less interesting, kind of constitutional history.

Since political history is the record of public events, the lives of the great men who took part in them, often made them, offer a very good way of studying it: a way not only attractive in itself, but more appropriate to the subject than perhaps in any other department of history. And naturally the lives of those at the very centre of events, those most concerned in directing them, will be of the greatest value and usually the most revealing. A biography of Lenin should be a ready and useful introduction to the history of the Russian Revolution; a life of Cromwell to our own seventeenth-century Civil War and Revolution. From such biographies as Pollard's *Henry VIII* and *Wolsey*, Neale's *Queen Elizabeth*, you will learn a good deal of the political history of the Tudor period. From such detailed 'official' biographies—which means biographies authorised by the representatives of the subject and based upon his personal papers—as Morley's *Gladstone* and Monypenny and Buckle's *Disraeli*, you will learn even more about the politics of the nineteenth century.

Constitutional history is much more impersonal;

and though it involves the lives of great men, and much light may be thrown upon it by their biographies, the biographical approach is not the appropriate one. Its subject is the history of institutions: an institution has a life and an interest of its own. I suppose it may be compared to the history of a species or a family in natural science; and those who like that kind of thing are apt to like it very much. But there is one word of warning here. The constitutional historians of the nineteenth century, Hallam, Cornewall Lewis, Erskine May, Stubbs, Maitland, were very much in touch with life and the kind of affairs they were writing about—public affairs and constitutional issues; Cornewall Lewis was a Cabinet Minister with experience of many offices, Erskine May Clerk of the House of Commons, Stubbs a bishop, and even Maitland—purest of scholars— intended a political career, which ill-health rendered impossible. And therefore their books have the feeling for public affairs in them, the sense of institutions and their way of working. Too much of constitutional history that is being written nowadays is by people very much out of touch with affairs, the denizens of libraries rather than of cabinets. They are apt to make the institution an end in itself, and their account of it too far removed from life—sometimes indeed, not to make any bones about it, quite dead and pickled. Now that is very different from Hallam's *Constitutional History*, which is filled with the sense of the living issues of the day; or from Stubbs, even though he got no further than the Middle Ages in his three volumes: Stubbs wrote from a large fund of common sense and experience of life, with great vitality and a wonderful sweep. Even Maitland, who was the *beau idéal* of the specialist researcher, was full of life and brilliance: he was indeed a man of genius and his investigations, the new trails he hit upon, often have the excitement of detective stories to the historian. He was the Robert Louis Stevenson among modern historians—and something more.

Maitland brings us to that fascinating borderland between constitutional history and law—he was trained as a lawyer—and economic history. These studies are close together and throw light on each other, especially in the Middle Ages; for so much of medieval economic history comes out of legal documents: much material for its agrarian history, for instance, is to be found in manorial records.

How are we to define economic history? Still more, how are we to distinguish it from social history?

I think it can be done. A rough-and-ready working distinction can be made by saying that economic history tells you how a society produces its livelihood, social history how it consumes it. Economic history is concerned with the ways and means by which a society gains its subsistence, its land system and methods of agriculture, its

69

industries, trades, businesses, its financial institutions, communications, conditions of labour and its modes of organisation and so on.

It is perhaps here that most new ground has been broken in recent decades. Just as the political progressiveness of the nineteenth century was reflected in an increasing interest in constitutional history, so the consciousness of the Industrial Revolution led to an enormous expansion in economic history. The phrase 'the Industrial Revolution' was popularised by Arnold Toynbee's book in the eighteen-eighties. Some of the most interesting of contemporary work is being done in this field, and some of the best of living historians are economic historians. There is R. H. Tawney, who writes like an angel—or an Old Testament prophet; G. N. Clark, who writes like an admirable eighteenth-century man of sense; Eileen Power, who wrote like the woman of wit and elegance she was; and there is C. R. Fay—the imp of inspiration that Kipling speaks of in his autobiography certainly sits on the end of his pen. Even more fruitful is the way in which the appreciation of the importance of economic factors has come into the field of vision of historians in general. We have all of us been affected by this—those of us, that is to say, who are any good.

"Economic history, the history of man's economic activity," Sir William Ashley tells us, "is the history of the utilisation by man of his environment, to obtain therefrom subsistence and the satisfaction of those material wants which are bound up with subsistence. But his activity in this direction, from the very dawn of history, has never been entirely individualistic; never altogether the operation of absolutely isolated individuals. Some form of association has always been in existence, it would appear, since man became man; and this has involved some sort, however rudimentary, of distribution of functions—some form, in short, of organization." Having said that, Ashley proceeded to write a short book, *The Economic Organisation of England*, which is one of the most illuminating books you could read on the history of our own country.

But there is the variety of economic history in itself, to which G. N. Clark draws attention. "There is, for instance, the history of technology, of tools and machines, of the chemical and other processes of production and transport. . . . It is a fundamental principle of the evolution of industry that a change of tools or machines brings with it a change of business organisation and of the human relationships which that dictates. Yet in finding out what the development of industrial technique has been, we must go far from the beaten path of historical studies. We must see the material evidence preserved for us in museums, and we must do archæological field-work in the often deserted and almost forgotten mills or forges of earlier centuries. We must visit modern mines, factories, workshops, farms. We must gather

71

information and ideas from engineers, from chemists, from geologists. For a long time the history of technology has had a life of its own. . . ." He goes on to discuss the newest fashion for 'business history,' which means "sometimes the history of separate firms or businesses, sometimes the history of business in a somewhat wider sense, of business methods and organisation. . . . There are business histories in the heroic or epic manner, of which the theme is the rise of the good man to riches. Others, such as the history of one of our great amalgamated banks, are largely genealogical, and provide useful information on the composition of the business classes in the last three hundred years."

It is obvious what a new field of work is opening up here. Quite recently we have been given the standard history of the Bank of England by Sir John Clapham; or there is E. T. MacDermot's fine history of the Great Western Railway. Or you may find a more human approach, less recherché and more rewarding, in such a book as Miss Sutherland's *An Eighteenth Century Merchant*.

Indeed the biographical approach offers as many potentialities in the field of economic history as any other, and may well prove the most promising to the general reader. For the writer it is more difficult; for he has to be skilled, or at least knowledgeable, on the technical side, as well as to present the personality of the subject; and these two capacities are not often combined.

You will often enough come across a biography of a technician—Dickinson and Titley's life of Trevithick is a case in point—which is adequate on the technical side, but jejune on the personal. You need to combine the two, in the way that C. R. Fay does in his *Great Britain from Adam Smith to the Present Day* or his *English Economic History*. In the latter he has an interesting chapter on "Desiderata of Industrial Biography." (Nobody could fill some of these gaps better than himself, by the way.) He analyses the various kinds of such biographies, those written from family piety, those written by the professional biographer who has no other profession than writing biographies—an unhappy type of book, fortunately in decline—those written by the technical expert and those by the professional historian. He gives us an example from each of the last two classes: Sir Alexander Gibb's *The Story of Telford* and T. S. Ashton's *An Eighteenth Century Industrialist, Peter Stubbs of Warrington*. He recommends these as "biographies which on any test are first-class" and from which "we may see the ground which a single biography can cover and how it weaves into the pattern of economic history."

And what wonderful figures and careers there are, full of energy, genius, achievement—sometimes of pathos, often of excitement and romance—in the lives of these inventors, bridge-builders, road-makers, engineers, capitalists. Kipling had

the sense of the excitement and creativeness of
their lives. What a wealth of great names and
great men of this kind we have had in our own
history alone—in fact a far larger contribution in
this field than any other country: Robert Hooke
and Newcomen, Coke of Holkham, Brindley, the
Duke of Bridgwater, Josiah Wedgwood, Ark-
wright, Boulton and Watt and Murdoch, the
Stephensons, Hudson the Railway King, Telford,
McAdam, Rennie, the Brunels, Cecil Rhodes and
Lord Nuffield, Sir Charles Parsons, the inventors
of Spitfires and Hurricanes and radiolocation.
There is no limit to the fascination of these men
and women and their lives and works, and no
reason why anything should ever be dull!

Trevelyan defines social history for us as "the
daily life of the inhabitants of the land in past
ages: this includes the human as well as the
economic relation of different classes to one another, the character of family and household life,
the conditions of labour and of leisure, the attitude
of man to nature, the culture of each age as it
arose out of these general conditions of life, and
took ever-changing forms in religion, literature
and music, architecture, learning and thought."
And he says roundly, "Without social history,
economic history is barren and political history is
unintelligible." Perhaps this is a bit too strong,
though it is an emphasis in the right direction;
at any rate, coming from the most admired poli-

tical historian of our day, it shows how strong a set there is towards a social conception of history. One can understand what it is in our time that impels us towards it, a time when the very foundations of modern civilisation have been threatened, all canons of social behaviour questioned, and society itself over large areas on the brink of dissolution. The problems of society are in the forefront of any twentieth-century mind, as those of political organisation were in the nineteenth century. Consciousness of society, with its problems, horrid and profound, is precipitated into the forefront of our minds. One agreeable by-product is a deepening of our sense of history, and the erection of what used to be thought merely decorative into a distinct and fruitful category of its own.

Social history has its own difficulties, though charming to read: its very continuity, the slowness and subtlety of its changes. Trevelyan tells us what they are: "Social change moves like an underground river, obeying its own laws or those of economic change, rather than following the direction of political happenings that move on the surface of life. Politics are the outcome rather than the cause of social change. A new King, a new Prime Minister, a new Parliament, often marks a new epoch in politics, but seldom in the life of a people. How then is the tale to be told? Into what periods shall social history be divided up? As we look back on it, we see a continuous stream of life, with gradual change perpetually taking place, but with few catastrophes. . . . In social history we find in every period several different kinds of social and economic organisation going on simultaneously in the same country, the same shire, the same town. . . . Each one, gentle and simple, in his commonest goings and comings, was ruled by a complicated and ever-shifting fabric of custom and law, society and politics, events at home and abroad, some of them little known by him and less understood. Our effort is not only to get what few glimpses we can of his intimate personality, but to reconstruct the whole fabric of each passing age, and see how it affected him; to get to know more in some respects than the dweller in the past himself knew about the conditions that enveloped and controlled his life." Having stated all the difficulties, Trevelyan goes on to create a masterpiece and set us all a model of how social history may be written, with his *English Social History*.

The subject flowers into all kinds of agreeable varieties, each of them affording specimens plain or coloured, exotic or simply inviting, and all rewarding to the life of the spirit. We have only space for a few examples. There is the history of literature and the arts. A few histories of literature are masterpieces in their own right: De Sanctis' history of Italian literature, for example, or Taine's history of English literature. Court-hope's standard *History of English Poetry* is alive at every point to the importance of social conditions: he rightly sees literature as the social expression it is and is well aware of the way in which even form and technique, let alone content, reflect the social circumstances, as well as the literary influences, of a period. This is true too of such admirable historians of literature as Sir Leslie Stephen and W. P. Ker: read two such remarkable books as Stephen's *English Literature and Society in the Eighteenth Century* and Ker's *Form and Style in Poetry*.

The same is true for all the arts and sciences: there are two ways of regarding their history and these have to be kept in focus. There is the history of the art or science as a technical discipline in itself—whether architecture or music, medicine or chemistry—and there is its history viewed as a product of a given society, reflecting its demands, needs and circumstances. You may see this approach in any good history of architecture—perhaps the most social of the arts, the art in which the social element is at its highest; look at W. H. Godfrey's *Story of English Architecture*, for instance, or the histories of many crafts, such a book as M. D. Anderson's *The Medieval Carver*. There is no end to the riches to be found here: you have only to dig a little and follow the lode.

In no subject has this approach become more conspicuous of late than in that of science—perhaps because it had more leeway to make up. The attitude of a group of the most interesting writers on science in our time—J. B. S. Haldane, J. D. Bernal, Lancelot Hogben, Julian Huxley, J. G. Crowther—is dominated by this conception of their subject, science as a social expression. It may well be that they push this view too far, at the expense of that which regards a science in the light of its own internal development. There is in fact no necessary conflict between them; but the over-emphasis of these writers is understandable enough in the light of the virginal innocence of older scientists about the society their work so much affected. The history of science as such has its *doyen* in this country in Charles Singer, whose histories of biology, anatomy, medicine, and of science in general, are not only standard works on those subjects, but afford a most congenial approach to them for the non-scientist.

Or we may take such offshoots from this prolific, umbrageous tree as the history of manners and customs, sports, education, culture. In our own time we have been given by M. and C. H. B. Quennell a delightful series of histories of 'Everyday Things in England': occupations, crafts, objects in use, household implements. James Laver gives us delicious brochures on the history of dress and costume. Or, more bulky and substantial fare, we have the magnificent Oxford volumes surveying society at different periods: *Shakespeare's England, Johnson's England, Early Victorian England.*

These things may be taken to add up to the
78

history of culture, a category to which English historians have not much contributed. *Kulturgeschichte* we owe much more to the Germans; an unkind critic might say that they write so much about it because they have so little of it. But the real reason is that their age-long failure to achieve political unity made them look rather to linguistic and cultural unity—*Deutschtum*—for compensatory satisfaction. We owe one of the masterpieces of *Kulturgeschichte* to a Swiss, Burckhardt's *Civilisation of the Renaissance in Italy*. A distinguished example of this kind in our own time is Huizinga's *The Waning of the Middle Ages*: a Dutch scholar, situated on the frontiers of national cultures, like Burckhardt at Basel, is in a favourable situation for observing their characteristics and what they have in common. Civilisation transcends frontiers: it is a plant of hardy growth: it survives a great deal. Perhaps we may regard cultural history as going back to Voltaire's *Siècle de Louis XIV*.

We cannot consider Spengler's *Decline of the West*, which had such *réclame* after the last war, as a true specimen of this kind of history. Apart from the fact that it has greater pretensions—altogether bogus, by the way—to exhibit a morphology of culture, it is utterly tendentious and inspired by the gloomy genius of German *Schadenfreude*. Because the Germans were defeated, Western civilisation is to be regarded as coming to an end: such is the simple motive behind that vast façade.

So characteristic of so many expressions of the German spirit, at once too obvious and too childish.

The best way to read the history of one country is as part of the civilisation to which it belongs: of this country and France, for example, as part of Europe, with all their many actions and inter-actions upon each other. There are books which will give you a valuable cross-section of history in this way, such as Tout's *England and France in the Hundred Years' War*, or C. H. Haskins' *The Normans in Europe*. But reading history across the frontiers demands more knowledge and is a sophisticated approach: it is perhaps a thing to aim at and grow up to, rather than a starting-point. The ordinary reader finds it easier to read foreign history as something foreign, external to ourselves: it is more manageable, if not more comprehensible that way. Diplomatic history, or international history as it is coming to be called, gives us a bridge. Its great defect is that it is apt to be boring and colourless, all in one dimension: the story of endless negotiations and intrigues, of memoranda and diplomatic conversations. Nothing more wearisome and fruitless. The most congenial way of tackling this rather uncongenial subject is the biographical. The lives of Foreign Secretaries and ambassadors are not without their lighter moments and are more human than the history of policy as such. I should not recommend you to begin with *The*

Cambridge History of British Foreign Policy and the works of Temperley and Webster on Castlereagh and Canning: you may go on to them. Better to begin with Duff Cooper's *Talleyrand* and Guedalla's *Palmerston*.

A deeper bond between one country and another, one age and another—a vast subject in itself—is Church history. Where are we to place it in our scheme? It is very difficult to say; for it impinges upon, or rather includes, every other kind of history, political, constitutional, economic, local, biographical, intellectual, cultural. It has an inexhaustible interest, and nearly all the great historians have either written about it directly or had to deal with it in the course of their work: Gibbon, Hume, Macaulay, Stubbs, Froude, Maitland, besides the historians—and those not the least distinguished—who have made it their special field. The fact is that religion is not only closely bound up with society, but has usually been one of the strongest of all bonds holding society together, in some periods as strong as the state itself. It has the further interest of a certain duality; for regarded from the point of view of society it provides the link between the secular, temporal activities of man and that other world, a timeless order, which is the reflection of the struggle of man's spirit in this. How can the history of religion, of the churches, be any other than fascinating? It deals with the lives of the most exquisite spirits among men: in our own history such men as Bede and Anselm and Grossetête, Thomas More and Hooker and George Herbert, Baxter, the Wesleys, Newman. And its range is widest of all: in some periods, like the Middle Ages, it is virtually the history of civilisation, and at the other end, in the smallest unit, it is half the history of the parish: for in the mighty past, it has been coterminous with the life of man.

A bridge of another kind between our history and the outer world is that given us by the expansion of our people, with our institutions and characteristics, overseas. They are no less inheritors of our history than we are ourselves, and as deeply affected by it. The American Revolution was the upshot of centuries of struggle for liberty and self-government within this country; the ideas that inspired it had a long pedigree from the lawyers and political thinkers of the seventeenth century and earlier. Though with the success of the Revolution the United States came into being as a separate state, no one in this country regards their history as that of a foreign country, any more than Americans are regarded as foreigners. Their history is thought of, like their literature, as an extension of our own, even if we know very little about it. There is in fact an increasing interest in American history with us, and useful contributions are being made, particularly to the earlier periods. Lord Charnwood's Life of Abraham Lincoln is perhaps the best shorter biography; and Sir G. O. Trevelyan's *History of the American Revolution* is likely to remain a classic of the Whig point of view.

But naturally enough, it is in the field of Empire history proper that the greatest expansion has been made in the last two decades. Dr. J. A. Williamson has given us new lights upon the early stages of expansion overseas, upon maritime enterprise and the Tudor navigators, the early colonies and our sea history in general: his work is original, delightful and inspired by a fine sense of imagination. A remarkable body of work has come into being, the best of it from the Oxford school. There is the work of Sir Reginald Coupland, covering many tracts of the Empire, but the bulk of his original work bearing upon Africa. His little book *Raffles* and his more recent *Livingstone's Last Journey* are the best possible introductions to the history of British Malaya and Central Africa respectively. The general reader will find his *British Anti-Slavery Movement* and *Wilberforce* as fascinating as they are instructive. W. K. Hancock has given us a masterly *Survey of British Commonwealth Affairs*, the best kind of contemporary history, a difficult species. His work—since he is an Australian—reminds us that contributions of importance to this subject are beginning to flow in from Canada, Australia, South Africa, New Zealand.

We are led to mention world history, a category in which, with the exception of Toynbee's *Survey of*

History, English historians have not much ambition to shine nowadays. We must not forget however that the most popular Universal History in the Middle Ages was by an English monk, Higden's *Polychronicon*; while Sir Walter Ralegh's *History of the World* held the stage for more than a century and will always remain a quarry for great English prose. In the nineteenth century Ranke wrote a *Weltgeschichte*. I have not read it. In our own time H. G. Wells produced a celebrated *Outline of History*, an enterprise that deserves recognition. It has the characteristic qualities and defects of that writer: largeness of imagination, immense and lively energy, extensive sympathies of mind, along with real superficiality and vulgarity, an impatient ignorance in things of the spirit. He is the *Encyclopédiste* of our time *par excellence*. Still, the intention was a noble one: in his own words it was "to show that *history as one whole* is amenable to a more broad and comprehensive handling than is the history of special nations and periods, a broader handling that will bring it within the normal limitations of time and energy set to the reading of an ordinary citizen. This outline deals with ages and races and nations where the ordinary history deals with reigns and pedigrees and campaigns. . . . History is no exception among the sciences; as the gaps fill in the outline simplifies; as the outlook broadens, the clustering multitude of details dissolves into general laws."

But is history a science? Does it reveal general laws in operation in human affairs? These are weighty questions that require discussion. We can only say here that the natural impulse of the historian is towards the concrete and the particular:

> To see a World in a Grain of Sand,
> And a Heaven in a Wild Flower,
> Hold Infinity in the palm of his hand,
> And Eternity in an hour.

Chapter Four

History as Science and Art

AT the turn of this century there was a great
deal of discussion in this country as to
whether history was a science or an art. The
discussion had been going on for some time on
the Continent, particularly in Germany where
it became part of a famous controversy among
philosophers and historians, the *Methodenstreit*.
Over here it was brought to a head by Bury's
celebrated challenge in his inaugural lecture at
Cambridge: "History is a science, no less and no
more." He followed it up with the declaration
that "so long as history was regarded as an art,
the sanctions of truth and accuracy could not
be severe," and, even more rigorously, "I may
remind you that history is not a branch of
literature." York Powell, the Regius Professor
at Oxford, thought much the same thing:
"Modern history today, then, shall mean what
might perhaps be called the New History, as
distinct from the Old History. The New History
is history written by those who believe that history
is not a department of *belles-lettres* and just an
elegant, instructive and amusing narrative, but a
branch of science. This science, like many other

sciences, is largely the creation of the nineteenth century. It deals with the condition of masses of mankind living in a social state. It seeks to discover the laws that govern these conditions and bring about the changes we call Progress and Decay, and Development and Degeneracy—to understand the processes that gradually or suddenly make up and break up those political and economic agglomerations we call States—to find out the circumstances affecting the various tendencies that show their power at various times. Style and the needs of a popular audience have no more to do with history than with law or astronomy."

That point of view became the dominant one in the universities in this century and it has had important effects, both good and bad.

To take some of the good first. The insistence that history is a science, with rigorous scientific standards and methods, led to greater care and caution in ascertaining and stating the truth, to a watchful emphasis upon exact accuracy at every point, in examining evidence and arriving at conclusions from it, a constant awareness of the dangers of bias and attempts on every side to counteract it. Of course, all this made history much more difficult to write—at any rate, well—and much less interesting to read. On the other hand, since this point of view attached little importance to literary quality, it meant a great increase in the amount of history books turned out by people who did not know how to write. Never was there such a quantity of raw hunks of historical research, malformed, undigested, indigestible, as poured forth from the presses. One is reminded of Swift's contempt—altogether less deserved—for the antiquarian works of Madox, for whom he had been passed over for the post of Historiographer Royal.

There was a further advantage from the point of view of historical teaching and examination at the universities. 'Unscientific,' 'literary' history —the ideal reading for the leisured country gentleman—was apt to become a 'soft option.' Ambling through Gibbon or Hume, Macaulay or Carlyle, deep in an armchair with the feet on the mantelpiece, was no way of training the mind. Something more gritty and rigorous was necessary; something that might take the place of the grammatical and linguistic discipline of the Classics, now that history was coming to displace the Classics as the most popular Arts subject in education. As early as 1853, Froude, then at the beginning of his career and in time to become a most distinguished 'literary' historian, especially obnoxious to the scientific school, stressed just this point in an interesting manifesto in *Oxford Essays*. His contribution was a proposal for a History School, which should get down to the study of the Statutes of the Realm and of the documents and texts from which history is written. Under Stubbs, one of the greatest editors of texts, that came about at Oxford, and other universities followed suit. The growth of the history schools has been one of the marked features in university education since: thousands of students have passed through them. No doubt the training they got in accuracy, in assessing evidence and making up their minds upon it, in common-sense judgment about public affairs, must count for something in the life of our community.

But—in historical writing? Trevelyan thinks that "Macaulay and Carlyle themselves would have been even better historians than they were if they had been through an academic course of history such as they could have got if they had lived at the end of the nineteenth century instead of at the beginning." I wonder. They might have been less biased, more accurate; they would certainly have been less passionate, less coloured, less vivid. Perhaps nothing would have reduced such personalities as theirs to the carefully neutral grey tints of Gardiner, the dry, repressed anatomies of Firth. And yet Firth, as a person, was a most vigorous and humorous human being. The reaction certainly went too far.

Its most deleterious consequence was that it made a disjunction between academic history, which exemplified good standards of scholarship but was not read by the public, and the kind of history that the public fell for. If people with good university standards would not, or could not, write in such a way as to be readable, the general public fell into the hands of charlatans, the Chestertons and Bellocs—or rather it was the Chestertons and Bellocs that fell into the hands of the public! Nothing could be worse: the public got a completely distorted view of the country's past, or a reading of it that simply made nonsense: James II treated as a hero, the Revolution of 1688 as a mistake, Elizabeth as a pathological puppet in the hands of a Cecil, the Reformation—which in fact made our fortune as a people—regarded as a disaster. It may be said by a sceptic that the dominant tradition of our history is so strong that we can well afford for opposition views to be put forward. But—however silly they may be? Whatever nonsense they make? I should say that the proper aim of historical study is to get as near the truth as we can, putting what is to be said for the Reformation, or the French Revolution or the Russian, or the British Empire, as well as what is to be said against. And as one who has for some years read the scholarship papers of candidates for entry to the university, I know the kind of harm that can be done by reading your history from that kind of book. (Mind you: I am not saying anything against Belloc and Chesterton as poets, essayists, novelists; I have a great admiration for their work in those forms; they were men of genius—but they were not historians.)

In our time a salutary reaction has come about against the too rigorously academic and 'scientific' view of history: it no longer has the field to itself even at the universities, and once more the best academic writers are writing for a wider public. The historian who more than any other has won this battle is Trevelyan, who all his life has stood for this view. He has told us how the "reaction against 'literary history,' as it was scornfully called, was rampant fifty years ago, when I commenced historian." But following him, a whole school of writers has come into existence, John Buchan with his historical biographies, Arthur Bryant, a purely professional historian like J. E. Neale with his *Queen Elizabeth*, or Miss C. V. Wedgwood—all of them with a university background and academic standards, who yet are read with enjoyment by a wide public.

It is easy to see now what the main influences were that made academic historians insist upon the scientific character of their subject. There was the increasing insistence of a scientific age upon exactness, accuracy, objectivity: there was—somewhat paradoxically, in the light of these standards—the influence of German thinkers; most important of all, there was the immense and deserved, if somewhat disproportionate, prestige of the physical sciences with their astounding achievements in theory and practice to their credit. As Trevelyan says: "Science had transmuted the economic and social life of mankind, and had revolutionised the religious and cosmological outlook of the educated world. These astonishing achievements of physical science led many historians, fifty years ago, to suppose that the value and importance of history would be greatly enhanced if history was called a science, and if it adopted scientific methods and ideals, and none others." He then goes on to declare his own point of view: "I believe that this analogy was faulty. For the study of mankind does not resemble the study of the physical properties of atoms, or the life history of animals. If you find out about one atom, you have found out about all atoms, and what is true of the habits of one robin is roughly true of the habits of all robins. But the life history of one man, or even of many individual men, will not tell you the life history of other men. Moreover you cannot make a full scientific analysis of the life history of any one man. Men are too complicated, too spiritual, too various, for scientific analysis; and the life history of millions cannot be inferred from the history of single men. History, in fact, is more a matter of rough guessing from all the available facts. And it deals with intellectual and spiritual forces which cannot be subjected to any analysis that can properly be called scientific."

Now we have the two opposing points of view. "History is a science, no less and no more" (Bury). "History is not a systematic branch of knowledge" (Eduard Meyer). What are we to think as between them? What is the truth of the matter?

It is proper to point out here that the word 'science' in modern usage has become increasingly restricted to the exact sciences, those which on the basis of demonstrable truths or observed facts, systematically classified, are susceptible of general laws, from which reliable conclusions may be drawn from like premises. Of these disciplines the outstanding examples are the physical sciences. Originally the word 'science' meant knowledge or learning, or any branch of it; as in the usage, 'moral sciences,' or 'theological science' —though the conclusions to be drawn from the latter, whatever the premises, could hardly be regarded as reliable, still less foreseeable, for all the overtime put in by the prophets! But perhaps it may be that even the exact sciences are not so very exact? The discovery of new phenomena is always bringing about the recasting of the theory. And what of the social sciences, such disciplines as economics, anthropology, psychology? I can only say here that it is not desirable to restrict the use of the word 'science' to too narrow a sense. The social sciences have not the cast-iron regularity of the physics of the nineteenth century—nor for that matter has physics in the twentieth century. What *is* it that historians have in mind when they claim, or disclaim, history as a science? I think they have at the back of their minds an idea of exactness, dependable objectivity (though in an ultimate sense what objectivity is there even in physics?), a certain capacity for being systematised as knowledge.

Most of us would agree that historical research

and study profit from their methods being as scientific as possible, i.e. exact, rigorous, systematic. In modern historical study there has grown up a much more accurate testing of sources, altogether fuller correlation of evidence. What were but tools of the historian's trade have become subjects in themselves, like palæography or diplomacy, the study of handwritings, the forms of documents. Archæology has become a world of learning in itself, with its own scientific methods, and with inexhaustible new fields of information to add to history. Air photography aids in the campaign that the historian wages with the past, recovering every scrap that he can, as well as it does in warfare. There are the further aids that we derive from statistics, from economics and notably from geography.

Even so, even in the realm of historical method, there is a non-scientific element that is just as important. There is the feeling for the material such as any good craftsman must have for the medium he is working in, the potter for the clay, the mason for the stone, the needle-woman for the texture of her stuff. There is sympathy of mind, love of the subject in and for itself, that kind of understanding that tells you what to beware of and what to look for: one derives all sorts of unconscious aids from the practice of one's craft, as with poetry or gardening. There is in the end, intuition: that leap of the mind that suddenly suggests the explanation. One cannot analyse it psychologically here, even if it is possible to analyse it satisfactorily at all; but it is liable to come, one cannot foretell the moment, when the mind is in a certain condition of preparedness, sometimes when one has worked oneself to a standstill along purely intellectual lines. Perhaps it is analogous to Keats' 'negative capability': that condition of receptiveness when the subtler and more spontaneous apparatus of the unconscious comes into play and takes charge, in a fortunate moment crystallising what had been despairingly disparate before. Is it any different really from the way a scientific theory comes to birth? I am afraid these things are very complicated, and when one gets into them the difference between one thing and another narrows down. But if they turn out to be curiously alike at bottom, there is, as against the difficulty we have in drawing our distinctions clearly, the consoling thought of the unity of human knowledge.

And again, with regard to the *content* of history, the matter in itself, the situation is complex. I do not accept the exclusiveness of either Bury on one side or Trevelyan on the other. There *is* a scientific element in history; the point here is to isolate it and to say what it is and what it is not. History in any case is not an assemblage of individual facts without connection, a rag-bag of things that have happened anyhow. All historians, of whatever school, have drawn conclusions and made generalisations from what they were describing. That fact gives us a clue to what must be the nature of the subject: it is descriptive like other social sciences, anthropology for instance, but there are generalisations from the facts viewed in sequence. The facts of history are not isolated, concrete, like pebbles on a beach; they are connected by skeins of consequence in every direction. One state of affairs leads to another, arises out of an earlier one; they are connected causally. The fact that the cause is often not simple or unilateral does not mean that it is not there; it only means that it is more subtle and complex to disentangle and estimate. That again is one of the advantages of the social sciences; they are not rigid and schematic: they have the subtlety, the suppleness and flexibility of life itself. All that they have to offer must be viewed in terms of life: that is the ultimate reality and their final claim. Life is the *ultima ratio* of history, not something outside of it, some abstraction of the mind that yet makes transcendent claims, something invented.

Yet this does not mean that there are not systematic elements in history—because it does not form one system in itself, any more than life does. There are such elements, capable of scientific analysis: the population of a country, its number and character, is a matter of great importance in its history and to any historian writing it. How shall he proceed in the matter?

My answer is by two methods, which dovetail in with one another: one is intellectual and scientific, the other is intuitive and æsthetic. They do not conflict; they complement each other, they illuminate each other. There is the whole secret of history, of historical writing and study: it lies in its duality of vision, an intimate and constant two-mindedness, or, if you like, duplicity of mind. It does not study the world through a microscope or a telescope; it has two eyes always upon the subject, one analytical and scientific, the other selective and æsthetic. Gibbon has his statistics and his generalisations, but he also gives you the picture of life and the feel of the thing.

Whether the one element or the other predominates depends on the subject and what you want of it. The systematic and scientific element is at its largest in early human and prehistory. It is of greater importance in dealing with mass phenomena than with the individual. Though even with the individual there is a scientific element—why otherwise psychology?; and in dealing with masses, conversely, there is a value-element—how otherwise patriotism, loyalty, self-sacrifice? These things are complicated and difficult to disentangle; but that is no reason why we should give up hope of ordering them, relapse into an easy scepticism where there are no distinctions and no understanding the lay-out of things: or on the other hand, rush hopelessly to embrace one or the other of two exclusive choices. We have to carry both in our mind all the time if we are to understand history.

Back to population, the example we took. If we are to understand that factor in the history we are dealing with, we need some statistics and some ethnology—a little of each will probably go a long way with the historian. In any case it will be better than mere impressions—though impressions too have their place. The impressions of Herodotus, as anthropologists now realise, have a great deal of scientific value. Sir John Myres tells us that "History, in its common and more popular sense, is the study of Man's dealings with other men, and the adjustment of working relations between human groups. But there is a larger sense, in which Human History merges in Natural History, and studies the dealings of Man with Nature. . . . Man's prehistory merges in the pageant of the animal world, and of the planet-wide arena on which it has been in progress. Mountain and sea-basin too have their history. Their geographical distribution has varied in immemorial years. . . . To see how the stage itself was set for this pageant, we must look back beyond the moment when the first characters enter it. For it has been Nature, rather than Man, hitherto, in almost every scene, that has determined where the action shall lie." It is obvious that here the scientific element is at its highest: indeed there is no understanding of all that tract of history except through science: they are practically coterminous. In these early stages human history is determined by geology and geography. We reach back to "more strongly marked contrasts in the composition and structure of its rocks, which have so profoundly affected the habitability and the human prosperity of each component region, through the peculiar distribution of its plants and animals, and eventually of its breeds of Man."

History is not then solely 'a matter of rough guessing.' There are areas where we can do nothing but guess, for lack of evidence; there are other areas where guessing—or imaginative interpretation—is the appropriate technique. But over and beyond these there are places where the right thing to do is to collect figures, establish generalisations, observe tendencies which have something of the regularity of law. Nothing is more remarkable to a really discerning student of our own history than the dualism of English and Celtic characteristics in our people: the extremism, the vivacity and temperament of the one, the solid reliability, the dogged qualities, the sensitiveness and imagination, the sleepless sense of moderation of the other. There is no doubt, fortunately, which is the dominant. Anyone with eyes to see can observe these strains coming out in our people and in their history; and we can say that without involving ourselves in the sillinesses of racialism. The stock counts for something, and a scientific ethnology is the way to assess it.

Without going out of our depth we can see that in quite ordinary tracts of history some generalisation is possible. Take the effects of inflation or deflation upon the economic circumstances of a society, the social relations of classes. We can observe with some regularity in history what the effects of an inflation are and predict with some probability what they will be. An inflation disturbs and throws out of gear the accustomed dues from one class to another: that which depends upon fixed monetary payments loses and goes down economically; those groups whose assets are in real property, mainly land—particularly if their ownership is absolute and their capital at their own disposition and therefore flexible—gain hand over fist at such a time. We may see the consequences at work in this country during the Reformation period, or in France during the Revolution. The consequences of deflation are still more regular and observable: gain for the rentiers and for the holders of fixed securities and payments, restriction of production, unemployment. Debasing the currency is a well-trodden path historically, and its consequences are pretty predictable. There seems no reason why we should not regard Gresham's law as an historical law as much as an economic one.

There are other general tendencies observable

in history, not only in the economic sphere—though there they may be, as Bury thought, at their most regular—tendencies that approximate to laws. When peoples arrive at a certain degree of cohesion, strength and self-consciousness, it seems to be impossible for other peoples to hold them down permanently. That nationalism is an irresistible force seems to be a conclusion to be drawn from history. I do not wish to say that history has any one *terminus ad quem*: that would be to suffer from the finality-mindedness of people like Hegel who thought the final stage in the realisation of the self in the world was the Prussian State, or others, equally childish, who find it in the British Empire. That kind of mentality is just a lag-over from the theological way of thinking of an earlier age—theology with God left out! Yet even Hegel thought that there was a progressive self-realisation at work in history; and I would suggest tentatively, that in spite of all sorts of disillusionments and setbacks, there does seem to be an irresistible impulse towards self-government in human society. And I am prepared to draw the conclusion from my reading of history in the realm of practical affairs and to say categorically that it went against the sense of history for this country to go on with the attempt to govern Ireland in the nineteenth century: we were right to quit and we ought to have quitted it before. Similarly, we cannot resist the movement of the Indian people towards self-government in the future. They will be less well governed but they will be happier governing themselves less well. The impulse is irresistible; the only point at issue is how and in what circumstances we can best hand over. The same general law brought the attempts of Napoleon and of Hitler to rule the whole of Europe to nothing, and will do the same for anybody else who tries the same thing. The general conclusion I draw from European history is that no one power is strong enough to rule all the rest. *Therefore* the sensible thing (i.e. what the sense of history indicates) is some federal system that may enable us to work together in co-operation. On the basis of a knowledge of history we can look into the nearer future and see something of the shape of things that is emerging. And that knowledge is the best aid to knowing what we can usefully achieve in our turn.

We are here verging upon the fundamental question of determinism and freewill that crops up in some guise in every age and mental climate, though it usually has a theological colouring in periods given to theological speculation. We may hope to deal with it as it affects history in the next chapter. It is sufficient for the moment to point out that man's success—indeed his universal triumph, compared with other animals—is due to his learning how to conform to the necessities of Nature. In Nature's service is his freedom— if it is hardly perfect freedom. (Perhaps perfect freedom is only to be found in service to an idea, an idea of the non-existent.) As Sir John Myres says: "It is man's inertia, rather than any initiative, his obstinate reluctance to abandon a mode of life once adopted, his recourse to any compromise—'rather to endure the ills we have than fly to others that we know not of'—and, in the result, his unique ability to conquer Nature by reasoned conformity with Nature's ways, that differentiates him from all animals but those, such as horse and dog, in which he has apprehended and elicited faculties remotely analogous to his own."

The distinction between the mass and the individual has an importance for the discussion of how far there is a scientific element in history, analytical and intellectual, as opposed to the descriptiveness and intuitions of art. It is to mass-phenomena that scientific analysis is most applicable. The individual is largely unpredictable; but even he—still more she—is not wholly unpredictable. Otherwise there would be no point in psychology; or where would be the point in 'the knowledge of human nature,' universally admitted to be useful? If we know something of his desires, predilections, characteristics—still more if we know something about his complexes, for they reveal the operations of the sub-conscious—we know a good deal of how he is likely to behave. With the mass our knowledge is a good deal more certain; for with a large number of people, the individual differences and idiosyncrasies even out and they will behave very largely in accordance with the forces that impinge upon them. Threaten the survival of a nation and they will fight as one man. History is full of such instances: the Dutch fighting against Philip II's tyranny, against Louis XIV's threat to overwhelm them, the French against reactionary Europe in 1792. Humiliate a people and you can expect a fairly certain reaction. Put down the wages of a class of workers, or attempt to take away the property of a given social group: I think the reactions will be fairly reliable, though their character and effectiveness will depend upon conditions, the strength of the group, the resistance it meets with and so on.

What you are chiefly dealing with in the realm of mass-action in history—and that is to the fore in political, economic, social, constitutional history, in the relations of states—is the public aspect of people's behaviour. You are not concerned primarily with their behaviour as fathers or children, as sportsmen or clubbable men, as artists or cultivators of their gardens. All that belongs to the private sphere of their conduct, and hardly concerns history at all—except perhaps social history, and, even then, only for what it adds up to. But it is precisely in this sphere of the public behaviour of the mass that one can generalise best, and even forecast to some extent. If geology and history provide the background to human history, we may change the metaphor to liken mass-action to the warp and woof of the texture, individual action to individual threads woven into it. They may have different colours and even pursue an erratic course across the patterns, but they remain part of the texture. To vary the image: individuals cannot think themselves off the map, or rather they may think themselves off it (many with philosophical and other-worldly interests have done), but they remain all the same upon it. They are conditioned, even determined, by their physical and social environment. Man is a social construct: he is what race and country, region and family, church and school and friends make him. As such, he is susceptible of analysis and even a fair amount of prediction as to his general course, though its particular lines may be fluid and flexible within the pattern.

This, then, is the perspective proper to history in which to view the actions of the individual. There is a great danger in theorising too much about history: any particular 'theory of history' is liable to be too schematic: the point comes when the rich and undisciplined variety of human events is forced into the restrictive framework of the (very fallible) theorist. And that is to go against the very nature of history: the sin against the Holy Ghost. On the other hand, we don't want to fall into the too comfortable armchair of historical scepticism and say that there is no knowing how human beings will act or react, that there is no rhyme or reason in it, that there are no regular tendencies or rules and no generalisation is possible.

There is some system in history and it is at its highest when you are observing the movements of masses. Even the most sceptical of philosophers, Hume, thought: "What depends upon few persons is, in a great measure, to be ascribed to chance, or secret and unknown causes; what arises from a great number may often be accounted for by determinate and known causes." The 'laws' of history, then, are of the nature of statistical generalisations: in dealing with one individual little calculation is possible; in dealing with a great number, one may even draw graphs, as in economics—provided one takes one's graphs with a pinch of common sense.

Dilthey, the modern philospher most congenial to the historian—with the possible exception of Hume—drew a marked contrast between *Naturwissenschaft* and *Geisteswissenschaft*, between the natural sciences and the humane studies. He thought that the empiricists and positivists of the nineteenth century, Mill and Spencer and Comte, were wrong in assuming that the methods and presuppositions of the natural sciences could be transferred substantially unchanged to the human studies. Dilthey thought, Professor Hodges tells us, that "the human studies are knowledge in a sense in which natural science is not, because physical objects as known to us are merely appearances, while minds are 'real realities' known to us as they are in themselves. This is not an attempt to deny either the reality of the external world or the real triumphs of natural science in investigating it. There are obvious ways in which we know physical nature better than we know man or society. We can describe and analyse, explain and predict, with far greater precision in the former than in the latter, nor does our knowledge of nature depend in any degree upon human testimony borne by unscientific witnesses. On the other hand, we cannot enter into the being of physical things and processes as we can with human beings and societies, where sympathetic insight, based on the identity of nature between ourselves and what we study, enables us to appreciate not only the external movements and changes, but the motives producing them and their meaning for the people concerned. It is this which makes Dilthey call the human studies a knowledge of reality in a sense in which natural science is not.

"The data of history not only are manifestations of mind, but are perceived as such, and this makes an epistemological difference between historical study and natural science. The scientist observes things and processes, but perceives no activity in them, no dynamic relationships. What he learns of their causal connections is learned by hypothesis and experiment and remains in the form of abstract law. But the manifestations of mind are instinct with the life from which they spring and upon which they continually react. We cannot observe them at all without seeing them as parts of a dynamic process, and this is the very thing that is meant by calling them 'historical.' 'Mind understands only what it has created. Nature, the object of natural science, embraces that reality which is produced independently of the activity of the mind. Everything upon which man by acting has set his stamp forms the object of the human studies.' "

I think Dilthey makes too rigid a contrast between the methods of the natural sciences and of the humane studies. For we must remember that in the simplest and most fundamental way historical method and scientific method are one and the same. In both you proceed from the assembling of particular facts to generalisations, and from generalisations back to the facts. In both science and history you do not start from nothing: you begin with common sense and with a working hypothesis; as you go on you modify your hypothesis in accordance with the evidence. And so generalisation is built up and theories which illuminate the facts, in the light of which they may be interpreted and often gain significance. But always, in both science and history, the generalisation is subject to revision in the light of new evidence: it is constantly being moulded and remoulded in keeping with the facts.

It is this that provides the defence for the detailed research that many people question in the case of history. What is the use of all this elaborate research into the wardrobe of Edward II, they ask; or into the distinctions between one kind of seal and another, great seal, privy seal, ordinary seal or signet; or between one kind of writ and another? Of course it is important to keep a sense of proportion; and there are historians who do not have much of it, just as there must even be scientists with none or very little. But it does not seem to occur to the man in the street to question the use of the same kind of elaborate and detailed research, that may not be leading anywhere in particular, in the case of science. Whereas the whole point—and the defence for it—is the same in the case of both history and science: it is essential for the subject as a whole to establish absolute accuracy and complete information, or as near as you can get to it, in regard to detail and in all parts of the subject. That is a process which must always go on and be pursued : otherwise the generalisations are faulty, the subject as a whole must inevitably suffer.

To my mind this is a complete answer to those who question the use of historical research, or for that matter of scientific research. The case is the same in regard to both. I repeat that I am aware that some researchers view things very disproportionately; to some extent that is in the nature of things: workers engaged in intensive study of a very narrow field are apt to think it more important than it probably is. But you never can tell what may turn up; and, anyhow, they might not otherwise go on. The remedy is clear: it is best to have a good general view of one's subject as well as to do a piece of detailed research into it. One needs to keep the two in focus, and each will have a salutary influence on the other: the detailed research for being viewed in a wider perspective, the general approach for having the caution, the accuracy and exactness of statement generated by the experience of research. I am all in favour of the good academic historian being able to write for the general reader on one side as well as for his own professional public on the other.

To return: on the other side there are some branches of science where the methods of study are largely historical. For example, geology: the establishment of successive geological periods follows much the same method as that of historical documentation, only the documents are rocks and stones. Or in the case of palæontology, the study of primitive organisms: of which the whole purpose is to establish the succession of series, by methods which must be historical. And so we move into the sphere of prehistory and then history proper.

I think I have shown in this chapter that there is a *Naturwissenschaft* element in the study of history; that is to say, that there are areas of the subject where a scientific approach is appropriate, in studying the physical and geographical environment and their impact upon the human story, in analysing economic and social forces and their influence upon the configurations and behaviour of masses of men in society; in understanding many aspects of mass-action and even in the psychological interpretation of the individual.

But in the long run all these intellectual aids are but external; the inner spirit of history, the genius of the thing, is elsewhere: it is in the spirit of man, the flame of life itself. The appropriate rendering of that can only be given by art. Even Dilthey allows a large part to the purely intellectual and analytical element in the historian's labour, "testing the meaning and value of sources, filling gaps, resolving inconsistencies, detecting causal connections, and so working out a coherent and well-grounded narrative. But he is only doing on a large scale what we all do when we understand the sayings and doings of our neighbours." That is to say, the historian's business is, like the novelist's, to render life in its proper terms, by common-sense interpretation, knowledge of human nature from experience and understanding, by sympathetic insight, imagination. Still, "where imaginative understanding can be turned into or supplemented by causal explanation, this ought to be done, and if there is sense in speaking of the progress of history towards the rank of a science, it must mean in great part this very progress from imaginative to intellective apprehension, from the vision of what is natural to the recognition of what is regular. In so far as this process goes on, the gap between history and sociology will be narrowed, and the dream of the positivists, that history could ultimately be made into applied sociology, represents the goal of such an advance, a goal none the less genuine because it will never be fully attained."

In the end, as Dilthey thought, it is the imaginative process of understanding that gives life and meaning to the rest. For that is the way to apprehend life—and history records for us life as it has been lived by man. Its essence therefore is in the concrete fact, the manifold variety of events and happenings that once took place in the real world. The historian's business is to narrate them, to re-create them. To do that he needs to be an artist. The process of historical re-creation is not essentially different from that of the poet or novelist, except that his imagination must be subordinated sleeplessly to the truth. He must consent to be ruled by the evidence and never once go against it. It is an austere, a searching vocation.

But it is not for nothing that the way of intuitive understanding, of imaginative insight has always in the end been that of the great historians. Herodotus and Thucydides, Tacitus and Livy, Clarendon, Hume and Gibbon, Macaulay and Carlyle, were all great artists and among the greatest writers of their time. And however much they may be supplemented by scientific methods and acquisitions—the contribution these have to make will certainly grow—there will always remain history as an art.

Chapter Five

Historical Thinking

THE nineteenth century saw a profound intellectual revolution, the full effects of which are only being worked out in our time. It was intimately connected with history; it was indeed mainly concerned with history: we may say that it was historical in character. It brought about a new way of looking at things that was evolutionary by nature; that is, it regarded them as *developing*, in ceaseless process of change. The actual process of change was not fully understood; Darwin's particular theory of evolution by natural selection was one hypothesis as to how change came about in the realm of natural science. But the great advance was to think of things in terms of change at all, and not merely that, but to think of change as having causes. Trying to analyse what those causes are has been a chief object of intellectual effort in both natural and social sciences ever since.

It is impossible to exaggerate the difference this approach has made in every sphere. You can see it most simply if you take an eighteenth-century work on history and compare it with the modern approach. If you take, for example, Lord

Bolingbroke's *Letters on History*—very typical of the mind of his age—you will see that he thinks of successive periods as a series of water-tight compartments, with nothing to account for the transition from one to another except catastrophes or break-downs. No conception of development or progressive change at all. (I use the word 'progressive' to mean producing something different or new, not in the nineteenth-century sense implying anything necessarily better, or moving towards some given end or other.) But now we think of things as in a ceaseless flux; and though that makes them much more difficult and complex to grasp, we are at any rate nearer to understanding them, or at least describing them as they are.

The effects of evolutionary theory have gone much further than this, as everyone knows. They have been such as completely to recast our view of the universe, of man and his place in it, of the descent of man—the controversy about this last was merely the most spectacular phase of the discussion, the one that had most publicity-value at the time, so to say, and not necessarily the most important. It has had the effect of undermining the absolute claims of religion and metaphysics, of ethics and law. (It seems that in an uncertain world, only the absoluteness of æsthetics remains, and possibly that of mathematical and logical propositions.) The idea of God has been rendered superfluous ; those who wish to retain something of the old framework of thought have been reduced either to a very shadowy and tenuous concept removed to an abstract world having little to do with human affairs, or else to a virtual identification with the human, indistinguishable from practical humanism. (Mere superstitions, of course, remain.) The evolutionary view of the universe has brought us to an almost completely relativist way of looking at things. Is there any absolute truth to be found anywhere, and if so, where?

That is where we are now.

But there is no use running away from it; or trying to refurbish the old dogmas, half explaining them away, half polishing them up to look like new. There is no help for us that way. Nor is there any help the way of people like C. S. Lewis, or for that matter Karl Barth or the Catholic reactionaries, with their return to a literalist mumbo-jumbo—always with the implication, 'You *shall* believe what *I* say' (not necessarily, note, 'what I *think*'). The categorical imperative is, in these days, without authority.

No: we can only face our difficulties and try to think our way through them. No doubt in what I am going to say I am giving myself away. I cannot help that. There are too many writers whose chief anxiety seems to be not to give themselves away. The result is that they are no help to us. They merely repeat what is safe to say because it has been said before. But we do not know what they think, if anything. I can only say what it is that I really think about these difficult problems, however inadequate and provisional it may be. There is this to encourage one: that nobody at any rate has entirely satisfied my mind on these questions, or said the final word about them, and therefore I must try to think out the answers myself.

Back to Evolution and its relation to History! Some people seem to think that the study of history, the whole concept of history, was revolutionised under the influence of the ideas worked out, notably by Darwin, in the field of natural science. R. G. Collingwood thinks on the other hand that evolutionary ideas in science were developed under the impact of history. "History had by now established itself as a science, that is, a progressive inquiry in which conclusions are solidly and demonstratively established. It had thus been proved by experiment that scientific knowledge was possible concerning objects that were constantly changing. Once more, the self-consciousness of man, in this case the corporate self-consciousness of man, his historical consciousness of his own corporate doings, provided a clue to his thoughts about nature. The historical conception of scientifically knowable change or process was applied, under the name of evolution, to the natural world."

There is more in this emphasis of Collingwood's than is generally realised, though I do not go all the way with him. Marxists are in the habit of pointing proudly to the fact that Marx with his ideas of social evolution was at least co-eval with Darwin, and thought of himself as a kind of Darwin of the social sciences. *The Origin of Species* appeared in 1859, *Das Kapital* in 1867. But Newman's *Essay on the Development of Christian Doctrine*, with its interesting, if arbitrarily restricted, theory of the evolution of dogma, was published in 1845. But before him was Coleridge, and before him Herder. I only mention these things in order to make clear—as an historian should—that there is little point in trying to track down who was first with the expression of a new idea: every historian knows that new ideas crop up in various places at about the same time, as if in response to new demands upon men.

In fact, evolutionary theory in science and what has been called, modestly and sensibly in England, 'the historical method' (*Historismus*, or historicism, in Germany) are twin developments of the same fundamental movement in thought, which characterised the 'mental climate' of the nineteenth century. Bury saw that clearly. "The growth of historical study in the nineteenth century has been determined and characterised by the same general principle which has underlain the simultaneous developments of the study of nature, namely the *genetic* idea. The 'historical' conception of nature, which has produced the history of the solar system, the story of the earth, the genealogies of telluric organisms, and has revolutionised natural science, belongs to the same order of thought as the conception of human history as a continuous, genetic, causal process—a conception which has revolutionised historical research and made it scientific." He goes on to explain that "for history it meant that the present condition of the human race is simply and strictly the result of a causal series (or set of causal series)—a continuous succession of changes, where each state arises causally out of the preceding; and that the business of historians is to trace this genetic process, to explain each change, and ultimately to grasp the complete development of humanity." He points out that "the predominant importance of the masses was the assumption which made it possible to apply evolutional principles to history . . . for it is only when the masses are moved into the foreground that regularity, uniformity and law can be conceived as applicable." It will be remembered that this is the very point that I laboured in the previous chapter: it is pleasant to know that Bury had the same thought.

The most notable attempt to work out evolutionary ideas in the realm of social science was that of Marxism. And certainly it has been the most influential in the effect it has had intellectually in all kinds of fields, in politics and economics, in history, sociology, literary criticism, and even, with some writers, in natural science itself, where its application much bothered the mind of

Lenin. (He wrote a pretty unreadable book on the subject: *Materialism and Empirio-Criticism*: a work of dogmatism and intellectual tactics rather than a contribution to knowledge.)

To confine ourselves to the Marxist view of history. Neither Marx nor Engels ever gave a complete exposition of what they thought on this subject; they never even devoted an essay to it. And yet it underlies their whole point of view about politics and society. What we have are various passages in different works of Marx *en passant*, with some glosses on them afterwards by Engels. But these are enough to make clear their point of view, and in any case the works themselves are illustrations and developments of it.

The first point to grasp is that the Marxist view came into being as a direct reaction against Hegel's 'Idealism.' Hegel thought of the universe in an evolutionary way, but as the self-development and the self-realisation of the primal 'Idea.' His was an idealist philosopher's way of looking at things, and there never was a more transcendental philosophy that was more absolute in character or more totalitarian in its claims. Quite early on, in the rude manner of a clever pupil turning on his master, Marx asked: "Do these gentlemen think that they can understand the first word of history as long as they exclude the relations of man to nature, natural science and industry? Do they believe that they can comprehend any epoch without grasping the industry of the period, the immediate methods of production in actual life? . . . Just as they separate the soul from the body, and themselves from the world, so they separate history from natural science and industry, so they find the birth-place of history not in the gross material production on earth, but in the misty cloud formation of heaven."

This was a very salutary reversal of emphasis, and it shows how Marx's view came to be described as 'the materialist conception of history,' or 'historical materialism.' Actually Marx disagreed with the mechanical materialism of Feuerbach, with his dictum *Der Mensch ist was er isst* (Man is what he eats)—only a German could be so crude—and criticised Feuerbach's materialist view of religion on the proper ground that he had failed to perceive that man is the product of his social relations and that religion itself is a social outgrowth. Marx suggests, rather than creates, a much greater development of his view with the following: "In changing the modes of production, mankind changes all its social relations. The hand mill creates a society with the feudal lord; the steam mill a society with the industrial capitalist. The same men who establish social relations in conformity with their material production also create principles, ideas and categories in conformity with their social relations. . . . All such ideas and categories are therefore historical and transitory products."

That opens up some very searching questions,

which we must return to later. Are the ideas and standards which are brought into existence by a given set of historical circumstances at a certain time confined to those conditions and that time for their validity? Are we reduced to a complete historical scepticism? The actual influence of Marxism in practical affairs has been in part towards a sort of nihilism on one side, the product of scepticism with regard to absolute standards, and fanaticism on the other. The two are not unconnected, as can be seen by reference to the Nazis. Marx himself never said anything on this ultimate issue; though his own behaviour was the reverse of that of a man who did not believe in absolute standards, while it is equally clear that he was not intellectually a sceptic. Still his silence is disquieting; and any discerning student of Marx is impelled to the view that he was disquieted himself and that was why he kept silence about it.

For the present let us finish our sketch of his view in his own words: "With the change in the social relations by means of which individuals produce, that is, in the social relations of production, and with the alteration and development of the material means of production, the powers of production are also transformed. The relations of production collectively form those social relations which we call society, and a society with definite degrees of historical development. . . . Ancient society, feudal society, bourgeois society, are simply instances of this collective result of the complexes of relations of production, each of which marks an important step in the historical development of mankind."

All this, I fear, is very German. But then Marx was very German. The trouble with so many German Jews is not that they are Jews, but that they are so hopelessly German. This is the way Germans write and think—Hegel is far worse; one can at least see what it is that Marx is saying. To go a stage further with him: "On the various forms of property, on the conditions of social existence, there rises an entire superstructure of various and peculiarly formed sensations, illusions, methods of thought and views of life. The whole class fashions and moulds them from out of their material foundations and their corresponding social relations. The single individual, in whom they converge through tradition and education, is apt to imagine that they constitute the real determining causes and the point of departure of his action."

With this last point we may readily, indeed vehemently, agree. Ordinary human beings never think of themselves as social products, of what they are and do and think—in that order—as being largely conditioned, not to say determined, by the circumstances brought to bear upon them, the forces and factors, environmental and inherited, that have made them what they are. The more unconscious they are of this, the more conditioned their behaviour and what passes for their thinking. The more self-aware they are, the more chance they have of achieving a certain measure of freedom. Freedom for a human being consists in knowing the extent to which he is conditioned, and choosing his course accordingly. But there is at every point a limitation upon our choice. All the great minds have agreed about this. Marx says here: "Men make their own history, but they make it not of their own accord or under self-chosen conditions, but under given and transmitted conditions. The tradition of all dead generations weighs like a mountain on the brain of the living."

Perhaps Marx's point could do with a little amplification. He means that individuals think of themselves and their ideas as the initiators of action, instead of being mere agents or rather the channels through which it came about. A seventeenth-century Puritan thinks that the Puritan Revolution came about because the King and his followers were wicked malignants upon whom the Lord's elect were executing justice. The illustration is not quite exact, because in the idea of the 'Lord's elect' there is an element of determinism, and the Puritans did think of themselves as channels of a higher power operating through them. That was mere human egoism, however, of quite the usual sort, which meant by God themselves and their own cause writ large. But they would have no idea of the underlying economic and social forces in the age which bore them upward like a tide to success, and which were the real determining factors in their victory. Only a very rare and independent cross-bench mind would have seen that. James Harington in fact did; but then he was a doctrinaire Republican, whose independent intellect fascinated and solaced the King who chose him for company in the last months of his life. Neither side liked Harington: he understood too much for them: he saw through the pretences of both sides: he saw that it was all pretty much self-interest. He was a man outside ordinary human action. He is often spoken of nowadays as a precursor of Marx. As if that were his only claim to attention! His was a mind of original power and interest in and for itself.

Marx regarded technical inventions in the sphere of production as a most important agent of social change, as having something like the importance of selection by adaptation in natural science. He says in a note to *Capital:* "A critical history of technology would show how little any of the inventions of the eighteenth century are the work of a single individual. Hitherto there has been no such book. Darwin has interested us in the history of Nature's technology, i.e. in the formation of the organs of plants and animals, which organs serve as instruments of production for sustaining life. Does not the history of the productive organs of man, of organs that are the material basis of all social organisation, deserve equal attention? And would not such a history be easier to compile, since, as Vico says, human history differs from natural history in this, that we have made the former but not the latter? Technology discloses man's mode of dealing with Nature—the process of production by which he sustains his life, and thereby also lays bare the mode of formation of his social relations, and of the mental conceptions that flow from them. Every history of religion, even that which fails to take account of this material basis, is uncritical. It is, in reality, much easier to discover by analysis the earthly core of the misty creations of religion, than it is, conversely, to develop from the actual relations of life the corresponding celestialised forms of those relations." [I should interpolate here that these latter are, of course, the work of imagination, of the unconscious, and not intellectual constructs at all : cf. the medievals' belief in the angelic hierarchy that reflected for them the feudal hierarchy of life on earth. But it was not consciously thought out: that was its strength : its roots were in the life of imagination and belief. Only a rationalist like Marx would expect to arrive at it by thinking.] "The latter is the only materialistic, and therefore the only scientific method." [He means, to proceed from the real objective world to that of the mind.] "The weak points in the abstract materialism of natural science, a materialism that excludes history and its process, are at once evident from the abstract and ideological conceptions of its spokesmen, whenever they venture beyond the bounds of their own speciality." A shrewd hit that, and it has not lost its point in an age that has paid too much attention to the popular commonplaces of Jeans and Eddington!

We have now enough material to go upon: I am not writing a book about Marxism. What we can see here is that Marx did not think of man as a passive agent. He insisted that man makes his own history, but within certain conditions limiting his action. Can we say to the extent of determining that history? Up to a point, yes; or perhaps we should say, beyond a certain point. Let us take an illustration. We might say that if certain events had not taken place in our history—if Richard II had not been defeated and dethroned, if Edward IV had lived or Edward VI or Henry Prince of Wales, if Queen Anne had had a son to succeed her—the whole surface pattern of our history would have been different; and yet it is probable that the underlying story of England would have been much the same, our fate and fortune not so very different, for that depends upon much more profound forces at work—our geographical position and character, the economic endowment of the island, nature of the people, their social structure and so on. There is the issue, simply stated. The point is whether we mean by history the surface story, which is capable of infinite variation, or the underlying story which is profoundly conditioned.

I do not know whether this distinction has been made before by any writer; and yet it is for lack of it that there has been endless discussion, largely due to this confusion. Everybody is bound to recognise that there is illimitable possibility of variation in the surface events of history—or almost illimitable; but also everybody is bound to recognise that the fundamental story of a country —say, what it can do or not—is largely conditioned for it. For example, in the modern industrial age, it has been impossible for Italy, for all her efforts, to be a great power: she has neither iron nor coal. The efforts were therefore senseless: they went against the sense of history, and she was bound to be pulled back by that necessity.

This historical point of view has a great importance for politics. Constantly in human history we see some power inflating itself beyond what its real resources can stand, and then it gets brought back again to normal—i.e. what is in correspondence with its real resources— usually by way of catastrophe and defeat. In the modern world we have seen it happen in the sixteenth and seventeenth centuries with Spain, which over-exerted itself to dominate Europe and so brought on a decline that has lasted ever since. France under Louis XIV inflated herself beyond what she could really carry—and underwent defeat and much suffering. But again under the impact of the Revolution and the leadership of Napoleon, she took the opportunity of the divisions among the other European powers to establish a domination over Europe. In the nature of things it could not last. Why should anybody try—and bring on themselves such catastrophes? And yet in our time Germany has made two attempts—bringing what disaster upon herself in the process! Her success could only in the nature of things be temporary: it could last only so long as Europe was disunited and divided in resistance to her. She was not really strong enough to dominate the whole Western world, any more than Japan was to rule the whole of the East. Why should people attempt the impossible?

The answer is that they do not know the conditions that determine what they can do: they have no historical understanding. "Things and actions are what they are, and the consequences of them will be what they will be: why then should we desire to be deceived?" Such was the ultimate wisdom of one of the greatest of British philosophers. Perhaps we may see in that dictum the unsleeping sense of the possible, of what can and cannot be done, which has been the instinctive guide of the English people and is the clue to their success in history.

But all this opens up further problems. If people understood how their action was limited and conditioned, would they act at all? Too much knowledge is in any case a great discouragement to action. So much of human action is irrational, senseless, wasteful, purposeless. Without a large penumbra of irrationality, of bravado, of attempting the impossible, of embarking upon forlorn hopes, it might be difficult for human beings to get going at all. Such is the nature of human nature. And in an age which has ceased to devote its mental efforts to analysing the nature of God, what we are up against is the nature of man. In so far as men are discouraged from effort, or withdraw (so far as possible) from active participation in events, the pattern is changed. One can go no further here. What we can say, on the practical side, is that people could do with a great deal more of historical understanding than they have got. We need not worry at this stage with ultimate intellectual issues. Just a little more understanding of history would prevent them making quite such fools of themselves or bringing down upon their heads, upon intelligent as well as unintelligent, the catastrophes, the disasters, the suffering they do. We can say that, I hope, without involving ourselves in a fakir-like passivity, a Buddhist abnegation of all action.

The point I was making à propos of which this argument was developed was this: that it depends whether you mean by history the surface stream of events, in which case you belong to the free-will school of thought, or whether you mean by it the deep underlying tides and currents, in which case you are apt to be a determinist. I believe that with this argument I have for the first time shown that these two schools of thought are not mutually exclusive and contradictory; and thereby shown how pointless much of the historical controversy between one side and the other has been—all for lack of distinguishing what each side really had in mind.

Marx had nothing to say on this, because he did not arrive at the distinction. Therefore he left his view of history undeveloped and fragmentary. His good historical sense forbade him to commit himself to any development of his theory which was contradictory to how things come about in practice. ("At any rate I am not a Marxist" he declared at the end of his life.) So he indicated what his view was rather sketchily in the passages I have quoted, left it at that, and spent the remainder of his life applying it and carrying it out in economics and politics, in both theory and practice. Nevertheless his view of history was at the heart of all his work and action. After his death, Engels, by way of countering extreme interpretations, returned once and again to what Marx and he had meant. He said that they had not meant to claim an absolute supremacy for economic considerations over all other factors; that the actual form of social organisation is often moulded by political, legal, philosophical or religious doctrines. "It is not that the economic situation is the cause, in the sense of being the only active agent, and that everything else is only a passive result. It is, on the contrary, a case of mutual action on the basis of the economic necessity, which in the last instance always works itself out."

If I may come to the rescue of Engels, and of historical materialism, I think the position may be put like this. On the basis of the physical environment, geographical and economic, man acts. He makes his social environment, though its character will be determined in the last resort by the physical environment, which for the most part it is not possible for man to transcend, though he may in some degree transform it. On that basis, out of the mutual action and interaction, of an increasingly complex kind as society develops, other modes of man's social life are formed, religious and cultural, intellectual and æsthetic. But—and here is the point—there will always remain a continuing element of the original physical environment that is not transcended—one can't jump off the planet or even the island—and this remains a conditioning factor all through the subsequent processes of man's history. That is all.

We may distinguish two main phases in the development of the Marxist attitude to history —with the crucial importance that has had for their part in contemporary world-politics. In the first phase the emphasis was all on the import-ance of conditions; we may call it the deterministic phase. In the second, the emphasis has been all on man as the active agent in the historical process: the dialectical phase. It is all very natural and explicable. To apply a little practical Marxism: in the earlier period the Marxists were themselves under the pressure of social conditions, the objects of action; only with the Russian Revolution did they come to be able to mould conditions, to become the active agents of historic change. They found the latter altogether more agreeable: as Lenin wrote in the preface to *The State and Revolution*, which he had not time to finish: "It is more pleasant and more useful to undergo the experience of revolution than to write about it." (At least, we may agree, for those who come out on top: but for the others, even those who helped to make the Revolution: Bukharin, Radek, Zinoviev, Kamenev, Rykov, Smirnov?—the list prolongs itself indefinitely.) Anyhow, the change has been reflected in a marked change of emphasis in the theory.

What is the relation between man, the agent, and the environment? I have already indicated what Marx and Engels thought about it, in the previous pages. The process of action and interaction between one and the other they conceived of in terms of Hegel's dialectic. This may be described simply as Hegel's way of thinking of evolution in the realm of ideas: you take any proposition as your *thesis*; the reverse gives you its *antithesis*; the conflict between the two and its outcome, reconciling something of each in a new proposition, gives you the *synthesis. Schluss!* Behold the rabbit out of the hat! Such is the famous Hegelian triad. I fear nothing is more boring in modern thought—or few things more boring; and nothing has been more disastrous to Marxism than its attachment to the Hegelian dialectic. (It is Hegel that is the evil genius of Marxism: *there* is the cloven hoof!) Perhaps the dialectic was all right in its time: it provided a scheme within which the evolutionary process could be grasped conveniently, and one that was rather more subtle than a uniformly progressive development—it allowed for setbacks and reverses in the process, along with leaps ahead. It did not err on the side of 'the inevitability of gradualness.' (The Fabians, being English, escaped the influence of both Hegel and Marx; they were Darwinians.) What Marx did was to take over the conception of dialectical process from Hegel, who had used it to explain the development of ideas, and apply it to the world of actual events, in short to history.

That was all very well for its day. But that day was precisely a hundred years ago. It is time that the Marxists, like everybody else, did a little fresh thinking. True, most people have not got up to the point of knowing what all the fuss over Marxism is about. Marxism is certainly plumb in the middle of the most critical intellectual issues of our time, but we want to be able to improve on it, pass beyond it, go further ahead.

And this is what is wrong with the Marx
dialectic of history. In the first place—and this
a shattering fault—it is an intellectual formula
that is applied from outside to the rich diversity,
the almost infinite variability of history; it does
not arise from the phenomena, the facts themselves: it is a piece of *appliqué* work. That is in
itself a great defect. Any theory of history, to be
at all satisfactory, must arise from the nature of
the material. The same holds good for science.
In the breakdown of the transcendent claims of
metaphysics—a transformation which Marxism
has done something to advance and is in accord
with—there is considerable agreement that the
best way to advance knowledge is for the separate
disciplines, on the basis of their specialist information, to reach forward to the general and the
abstract; rather than for the general and the
abstract to impose their assumptions and pre-
conclusions upon the more assured knowledge of
the sciences, natural or social. The imposition of
the dialectic upon history is an obvious relic of the
old transcendent claims of idealist metaphysics;
and it is in complete contradiction to the implications of Marxism as an essentially historical doctrine. I do not know that this point has ever been
made before, but I am quite clear that if we are
to retain what is most valuable in Marxism—and
there is much—the dialectic has to go.

It is far too schematic, too rigid a formula for
the subtlety of history, where peoples and causes

are not only defeated and fall out of the process, but sometimes suffer, almost inexplicably, a failure of nerve and disappear. It is insufficiently supple or flexible for the infinite variety of historical phenomena, with all the ups and downs, the ebbs and flows and the innumerable coiled convolutions of human action within those processes that are determinable. Better to have a wise and wary scepticism than to rivet such an iron framework upon such subtly refractory material. Better to have no theory at all and trust to common sense in the English fashion than to sacrifice truth to a false theory. Actually I think there is no reason to be driven to scepticism; I have done my best to build up a theory that is in correspondence with the facts, and any theory of history must be one that arises from the phenomena.

Far worse and more flagrant is the practical consequence of the Marxist dialectic: it gives you no objective standard as to the sense or rationality of action. It becomes in practice a dangerous pragmatism—all the more dangerous because so ineffective, as well as misleading. And that this was so may be proved by the utterly senseless, as well as unscrupulous, record of Communist international policy between the two wars. The Communists made it their main end and aim to destroy Social Democracy, on the assumption that it would be Communism that would emerge triumphant. Capitalism being the *thesis*, Social Democracy the *antithesis*, Communism must then be the *synthesis*, the outcome of the conflict: so ran the argument. Could anything be more childish? You can always arrange the triad according to what you want to obtain from it, like manipulating the oracle. You might as well take Social Democracy as the thesis, Communism the antithesis, Fascism the synthesis: which was in fact nearer to what came about. Throughout the whole period of the Weimar Republic the Communists made it their main end and aim to undermine it, and directed their chief attack against the Social Democrats who supported it. The result was not victory for the Communists, but for the Nazis. I am not saying that other people were not to blame too, but the upshot of these lunatic efforts was that millions of simple good men died in the event. How often in these years one has thought of the cry of Shaw's St. Joan: "Must then a Christ perish in torment in every age to save those that have no imagination?" I do not go so far as to expect human beings to have any imagination; I merely ask for a little common sense, and a little historical understanding from those who set themselves up to be their leaders.

The plain fact is that the dialectic left its adherents with no standards of right and wrong in action, of what made sense and what did not make sense—except what was to the interest of Russia. A war, which in truth was waged in defence of civilisation and was a 'damned near thing,' was an imperialist war until the very morning of

Hitler's attack on Russia, when it became in that
moment a just and right war in defence of democracy. To such bankruptcy had years of deliberate confusion of means with ends brought the
Communists. It was a terrible degradation of
any standards of historical judgment, at least as
bad as that of those people in this country who
thought it possible to come to terms with the
Nazis. That too was always nonsense and showed
no understanding of history or any political sense;
but the Communists were sinning against the supposed light. A simpler point of view than mine
—or theirs—would condemn their behaviour as
morally wrong, indeed criminal. But our business is with historical judgment here, not with
ethics. And I content myself with saying that
their whole record in that period did not make
sense historically. (They did not even succeed in
killing Social Democracy. We have been through
a great war which might never have been
brought down upon us if the international unity
of the working-class had not been destroyed—and
at the end of it Social Democracy is very far from
having disappeared!) In history the proof of the
pudding is in the eating. But one ought not to
need ten or twenty years to tell what it is going
to be. Anyone with a good knowledge of history
and a common-sense judgment of how human
affairs proceed could have told beforehand how
fatal this course of action would be. It can be
seen in historical retrospect in such a book as

A. J. P. Taylor's *The Course of German History*; it is true that that is *ex post facto*; but I may claim that the way things would turn out is pretty clearly indicated in the political essays I wrote before the event.

I am not blaming all this upon Marxism as a body of thought, still less upon historical material- ism as sketched by Marx and Engels, but upon the narrow and sharpened 'dialectical material- ism' that was developed from Lenin onwards. The historical outlook of Marx and Engels was a much wider and more catholic thing than the orthodoxy of their Communist followers. It may be said that Social Democracy has inherited the broader and more catholic interpretation of Marxism. Here we are only concerned with its influence on the conception of history and historical writing. As such, taken at its broadest and best, it has had a stimulating and fruitful influence—immense on the Continent, and even at last beginning to show signs in England. One can go so far as to say that to be a good historian in our time one needs to have been something of a Marxist. One needs to know what it is all about, to have seen the point of it, to have felt the influence—even if one comes out the other side. Croce came out the other side, but he had under- gone something of the influence of Marx, though still more that of Hegel. Apart from orthodox Marxists, one can see the influence at work with such eminent historians as Rostovtzeff and Vino-

Iradoff; and in this country, R. H. Tawney and G. N. Clark.

Marxism, like any other form of evolutionary thought, brings us up against the question of historical relativism, or historicism (*Historismus*). This is the problem that lies at the heart of historical thinking, and to which the most eminent minds of our time in this field have addressed themselves, Dilthey, Troeltsch, Croce—I cannot think altogether satisfactorily. No one in this country has taken up the discussion; perhaps not many are conscious of its crucial importance.

We had an example of the way the problem opens up when we mentioned the change of emphasis in Marxist thought from determinism to activism with Lenin and the Russian Revolution. It is a good example of the way theory adapts itself to new needs, changed conditions. But which is true? Is there any way of arriving at a view that is true for all conditions? Are we not reduced to a purely pragmatic attitude to truth?—you change your view of what is true according to your needs.

That is the great intellectual problem—I had almost said disease—of our time. One can see its ravages on all hands in the confusion of the Communists between means and ends in political action, and the consequent senselessness of much of their record from the point of view of achieving even their own objectives; in the criminal and deliberate nihilism of the Nazis, the cheap Machiavellianism of the Fascists (the Duce gained his doctorate in the university of Perugia with a thesis on Machiavelli); one can see it no less in the scepticism, the Laodiceanism in action, of good men who find the problem too much for them and give up any endeavour to bring an ordered body of thought out of the welter of contemporary experience and knowledge. Others think to stay the ravages of contemporary relativism—the decline of belief in absolute standards, the psychological undermining and questioning of all motives and so on—by a crude reassertion of the very doctrines, religious or metaphysical, that have been found wanting. That is no way to help us. We have to accept the new and profounder knowledge our time has brought us, with the new and deeper doubts—and surmount them; if possible achieve a synthesis.

Let us look at how the problem struck a few choice spirits. Burckhardt, the historian of culture, was one of the first to sense it. "History is actually the most unscientific of all the sciences, although it communicates so much that is worth knowing. Clear-cut concepts belong to logic, not to history, where everything is in a state of flux, of perpetual transition and combination. Philosophical and historical ideas differ in essence and origin; the former must be as firm and exclusive as possible, the latter as fluid and open. . . . Nothing wholly unconditioned has ever existed, and nothing that was solely a determinant. At the same time, one element predominates in one aspect of life, another in another. It is all a question of relative importance, of the dominant at any particular time." Burckhardt did not go any further than that; the tendency of his mind was sceptical, though full of ripe reflections. A practical deduction that he drew was that in judging the men of a particular epoch with their virtues and vices we must see them "within the system of their time." It is a part of the historic sense to be able to judge an age in relation to its needs, its problems and achievements, to set its failures against the satisfactions given. But he did not go further to draw any implications other than this limited practical one.

Morley did, towards the end of his life, in an interesting lecture, *Notes on Politics and History*. After describing what he calls 'the historic method,' he says: "It is easy to see that the ascendancy of the historic method has its drawbacks. Study of all the successive stages in beliefs, institutions, forms of art, only too soon grows into a substitute for direct criticism of all these things upon their merits and in themselves. Inquiry what the event actually was and what its significance and interpretation becomes secondary to inquiry how it came about. Too exclusive attention to dynamic aspects weakens the energetic duties of the static. More than one school has thus seen the predominance of historic-mindedness excessive. It means, they truly say, in its very essence, veto of the absolute, persistent substitution of the relative. Your method is non-moral, like any other scientific instrument. There is no more conscience in your comparative history than there is in comparative anatomy. . . . Talk of 'eternal political truths,' or 'first principles of government,' has no meaning. Stated summarily, is not your history one prolonged 'becoming' (*fieri, werden*), an endless sequence of action, reaction, generation, destruction, renovation, 'a tale of sound and fury signifying nothing.' Such argument as this, I know, may be hard pressed, and it is in truth a protest for the absolute that cannot be spared to many active causes. But that relative tests and standards are the keys both to real knowledge of history, and to fair measure of its actors, is a doctrine not likely to lose its hold."

In short Morley knew what the argument was about, and funked it.

Dilthey realised all its implications and formulated his answer. Professor Hodges, in a summary of Dilthey's position, says: "This widening of consciousness through historical knowledge has disconcerting results. Every age expresses its attitude to life and the world in certain principles of thought and conduct, which are regarded in that age as absolute and unconditionally valid. . . . The historian discovers these principles in every age which he studies, but he also discerns that they vary from age to age, and that, in spite of the claim to absoluteness which is always made, changed circumstances always result in changed principles, which are therefore historically relative. . . . History having recorded the relativity of all ideas and practices, points to its own relativity, and leaves us in the position known as historicism, or historical relativism. Dilthey recognises this, and there is evidence that he was visited by occasional twinges of nervousness at the blank prospect which it opens up—a prospect which has led many in the present age to cynicism and apathy, and caused others to seek escape in dogmatic obscurantism and authoritarianism. There are some, however, who have found it possible to look historicism in the face and yet avoid discouragement, and in spite of occasional doubts, Dilthey was one of these. He not merely admits the necessity of historicism, he proclaims it and regards it as a source of freedom and inspiration.

"How can he do this? Because he sees historicism first of all as a deliverance from superstition and illusion, and secondly as a revelation of the manifold capacities of human life. If our grandfathers reacted to their situation in one way and we react to ours in another, the conclusion which Dilthey draws is not that no one can ever know how to act or think, but that in every situation man can find a way. . . . And the more we learn that every particular set of principles is the mind's reaction to a particular set of circumstances, the more it appears that even historicism has to admit one absolute after all, viz. the marvellously adaptable human mind itself."

It will hardly escape attention that this, though very interesting and suggestive in itself—and though we may agree with it—is not a satisfactory answer. It is an answer on the practical plane; it tells us something of the uses of historical thinking, but does not tell us how far its categories are valid—whether what it tells us is true.

What about Croce? (Collingwood, a brilliant writer, who passes in this country for an original thinker, derives his thought from Croce.)

Croce tells us that "historicism (the science of history), scientifically speaking, is the affirmation that life and reality are history and history alone. The necessary corollary to this affirmation is the negation of the theory which holds that reality can be divided into super-history and history, into a world of ideas and values and a lower world which reflects them." [He means that events and ideas are all part of the flux of history.] "The quick of this argument lies in the demonstration that the ideas or the values which have been taken as the measure and the models of history are not universal ideas and values but are themselves particular and historical facts elevated to the rank of universals." Here again we observe the sceptical note that proceeds from all who are affected by historical relativism. Croce is quite right when he says that the historical outlook completely undermines a superficial rationalism, of the eighteenth- and nineteenth-century type, and in its place develops a profounder rationalism, which, realising how irrational men and events are, would on the basis of that knowledge the more satisfactorily subsume them and shape them into order. Leadership of the irrational by the rational is the end, not the old superficial denial of irrationality: its discovery, or at any rate the discovery of its preposterous extent, by modern psychology should be a great aid to its enlistment in the service of reason and sense; indeed, it is a necessary condition. It is that aspect of the extension of knowledge in our time that gives us most hope.

Croce, who has spent a good deal of his life in philosophising and has written many large works on the subject

    (Lie heavy on him, earth, for he
      Laid many a heavy load on thee)

now aligns himself with those who see no place for metaphysics. "The conclusion that philosophy serves no other purpose than as a 'methodology of historical thought' has often been formulated and doctrinally demonstrated by me to the great displeasure of the so-called pure philosophers." In the belief that philosophy is merely good sense, he asks "whether there is anything else to be known in the world other than the events among which we live and have to work, and whether philosophic reflection can ever be justified as anything but a way or method by which to achieve this sole effective and useful knowledge." In fact, he has already told us in a chapter entitled "Historical Knowledge Considered as Complete

Knowledge": "It is not enough to say that history is historical judgment, it is necessary to add that every judgment is an historical judgment or, quite simply, history. . . . Historical judgment is not a variety of knowledge, but it is knowledge itself; it is the form which completely fills and exhausts the field of knowing, leaving no room for anything else."

Now we know where Croce's disciple, Collingwood, got the conclusion of *The Idea of Nature* from. He is arguing that scientific work is in essence historical. "The scientist who wishes to know that such an event has taken place in the world of nature can know this only by consulting the record left by the observer and interpreting it, subject to certain rules, in such a way as to satisfy himself that the man whose work it records really did observe what he professes to have observed. This consultation and interpretation of records is the characteristic feature of historical work. Every scientist who says that Newton observed the effect of a prism on sunlight, or that Adams saw Neptune, or that Pasteur observed that grape-juice played upon by air to a certain temperature underwent no fermentation, is talking history. The facts first observed by Newton, Adams and Pasteur have since then been observed by others, but every scientist who says that light is split up by the prism or that Neptune exists or that fermentation is prevented by a certain degree of heat is still talking history: he is talking about the whole class of historical facts which are occasions on which someone has made these observations. Thus a 'scientific' fact is a class of historical facts; and no one can understand what a scientific fact is unless he understands enough about the theory of history to understand what an historical fact is. . . .

"I conclude that natural science as a form of thought exists and always has existed in a context of history and depends on historical thought for its existence. From this I venture to infer that no one can understand natural science unless he understands history: and that no one can answer the question what nature is unless he knows what history is. This is a question which Alexander and Whitehead have not asked. And that is why I answer the question 'Where do we go from here?' by saying, 'We go from the idea of nature to the idea of history.'"

At that point Collingwood died. And perhaps no wonder. It is difficult to see how he could have gone any further. It is also remarkable how obtuse clever men can be. Of course, in a sense, history underlies everything. It is obvious that everything has an historical aspect. But that does not mean that history *is* everything. And there is surely a plain confusion of thought beneath what Collingwood says. The real essence of scientific investigation is not the "consultation and interpretation of records," as in history; it is in verification by experiment. (There is an analogous

148

'verification by experiment' in history, where, as I have said, the proof of the pudding is in the eating. But this is *ex post facto*; you cannot test it out beforehand, there are too many imponderables in the equation.)

It seems to me that Croce and Collingwood land themselves in an historical mysticism as dangerous as any pragmatism—dangerous because it does not distinguish between things. Croce identifies the judgment of events with the knowledge of their genesis: "the concept that concrete and true knowledge is always historical knowledge has the obvious consequence that the knowledge or qualification or judgment of an event cannot be separated or distinguished from the knowledge of its genesis." But origin is not the same thing as validity, nor is knowledge of the origin the same thing as judgment of it. Croce goes too far in his *mystique de l'histoire* when he tells us: "Reality is history and is only historically known. The sciences certainly measure it and classify it as is necessary, but properly speaking do not know it, nor is it their business to know its intrinsic nature." He ends by identifying humanism with the historical outlook. "The heir of this great labour is historicism, which contains in itself liberation from transcendence of all kinds, affirmation of moral, political and economic life, emphasis upon passion and poetry, rejuvenation of intellectual and moral life, dialectic which is its new logical instrument."

We may agree with Croce that historical think-ing liberates us from the transcendental, and with his polemic against the wholesale intrusion of ethical judgments from one age and clime into totally different ones. "Those who on the plea of narrating history bustle about as judges, condemn-ing here and giving absolution there, because they think that this is the office of history, are generally recognised as devoid of historical sense." This gives short shrift to Acton with his famous dictum, "Power tends to corrupt, and absolute power corrupts absolutely." And indeed it is too simple and summary: the code of a high-minded Victorian gentleman applied to the welter of his-tory. But does that mean that one can apply no ethical standards to history? I think not. Very well, what standards are there? Croce gives us a hint in a passage which contradicts much of what he has said before, when he says, "Since every affirmation is a judgment, and judgment implies category, the constitutive element of historio-graphy is the system of judgment-categories."

We have seen that if you follow the principle of dialectic you have no external standards of judg-ment at all, they are one with the process. My personal view of this appallingly difficult question is this. The standards or categories must arise from the nature of the phenomena you are study-ing, whether historical or scientific. They form something of a system in accordance with your experience of life and in accordance with their own logical coherence, by both of which they must be tested all the time, constantly. Standards which can be applied to history, which are appropriate to history, arise therefore out of history. Many courses of action condemn themselves, and not only by disaster or failure: they may be criminal or immoral. Such judgments are possible, as I hope to show immediately. Many men in history condemn themselves, or conversely are to be admired and praised. Of course we must understand them and *their* standards in terms of their age and *its* standards. But are those standards or values completely transcended by time? They certainly have a time-element in them, and the time-element is greater in, say, political and ethical standards than it is in æsthetic or purely intellectual—in mathematics or pure logic for example. One might almost construct a hierarchy of values, from those which are most subject to changing conditions to those which are least.

When we look into these standards we see that they have not only an element that comes from the changing conditions of the time, but also a more permanent element which relates to something continuous and enduring. Let us take a Greek tragedy: a good deal of it reflects the social conditions of a vanished age, its standards of judgment; but enclosed within that envelope there are æsthetic values that speak to us for all time—or at any rate so long as man is recognisably man. There are things of beauty—and probably as Burckhardt and many others have thought (Robert Bridges and James Joyce among them) æsthetic values are more constant than any—that come across to us still with undiminished force. But it would not be common sense to deny that there are other values that come across to us too with authority and command our assent—ethical values. For the plain fact is that underlying all the flux and change of history, the mutually contradictory claims of religions, the parochial squabbles of the sects for our allegiance or our cash, the indisputable tendency of individual egoism to assert itself as universal—underneath all the change of circumstance and condition there is a certain continuum to which all standards may be related for their validity: the nature of man *quâ* man. It is that that gives substance, a real basis to our moral judgments, however conditioned by time, so that we may as historians condemn Nero for a bad man and acclaim Jesus Christ as a good man.

A modern philosopher like Professor Stebbing says: "Even if ethical principles are eternal and immutable it is certain that they need to be re-interpreted for every period and re-thought for every generation. Our moral beliefs, our standards of right and wrong, our conception of our relations to other men undergo some change as our modes of living change." She tells us that it is a mistake to deduce morals from metaphysics; that "morality is not to be deduced from anything else; the concept of moral obligation is not to be exhibited as a deduction from a system of the universe. On the contrary, the fact that we know what it is to be morally obliged is a datum that must be fitted in, if we are so ambitious as to construct a theory of the universe."

All this fits in, from the side of a contemporary philosopher, with the knowledge that accrues to us from history and the historical method. We are not left with a complete scepticism about everything, as the result of our experience of historical relativism. We *can* build up a body of knowledge, from which we can tell, for example, in one sphere that it was always nonsense to try to appease the Nazis—it was contrary to the nature of a régime whose whole inner logic was aggression and conquest; or again, to hold that there can be a future for the Liberal Party in this country, when its whole social and economic foundation has given way. Historical thinking can tell you both these things; or to take an example from a different sphere: that the Christian doctrine of love among men is a better basis for human relations in a society than envy and hatred. And that without subscribing to any metaphysical propositions of a quite incredible kind.

This body of knowledge that we build up out of history does relate to the needs and times we live in; and of course there must be a constant process of adaptation of knowledge to the time. A great deal of earlier knowledge is constantly

being rendered out of date, like much of early
science, astrology, alchemy—having served its
purpose in developing astronomy and chemistry
—or for that matter theology or political and
economic thought. But we draw out of it all that
which we need, that which lasts, stands the longer
tests of time and relates to the enduring continuum
of man's experience as man. The way to truth
then is to understand these changes in accordance
with changing conditions, to pierce through to
the underlying continuity of knowledge and experience. Historical thinking is the appropriate
method. For knowledge too has had its own
continuum no less than experience: it is not
merely pragmatic, yielding temporary answers to
temporary questions, nor merely utilitarian, to be
discarded out of mind. It may be forgotten—and
come up again after centuries. It is perpetually
being remade and remoulded to our needs, of
which some are practical, others intellectual,
such as the universal human need to get coherence
out of what we think, reduce to rational order
what we experience.

However relativist the historian, he can then
agree with the philosopher that there is positive
knowledge: "It is an illusion to find the value of
our lives here and now in a life to come; it is an
illusion to suppose that nothing is worth while for
me unless I live for ever; it is an illusion to suppose
that there is no uncompensated loss, no sacrifice
that is without requital, no grief that is un-

assuaged. But it is also no illusion but uncontested fact that here and now we know that hatred, cruelty, intolerance, and indifference to human misery are evil; that love, kindliness, tolerance, forgiveness, and truth are good, so unquestionably good that we do not need God or heaven to assure us of their worth." [1]

No: those values emerge from, and rest upon, the positive experience of man in history.

[1] L. Susan Stebbing, *Ideals and Illusions*.

Chapter Six

History and Education

IT is evident that history is a subject of superb educational value. Yet it seems that that is little enough understood by the general public, or, by those who do not question its value, why it should be so.

Let me give an admittedly extreme example, one so idiotic as to serve as a *reductio ad absurdum* of the hostile view.

At the universities history has become in our time the leading arts subject—it has taken the place of the Classics in the last century. Most of my readers will know, what I know as a tutor from sad experience, that so far as the universities are concerned the war has fallen with peculiar hardship upon the arts students—students of history, languages, classics, law, the social sciences; in fact it may be said to have been fought in their lives. Science men and medicals were reserved and could take their full course of study; and even when in the Forces they could to some extent, for war purposes, carry on with their professional training. The result of this disparity has been very serious for the arts subjects. It is especially serious for the professions, for which arts students at the universities are the recruits: for the educational services, the churches, the Civil Service, home, foreign and colonial, local government and the growing body of social services, for the legal profession and all the literary professions, writing, publishing, journalism. Everyone knows that in all these callings there are urgent shortages of recruits—for six years only a trickle has been passing through the universities; and in view of the training necessary to equip them for their job in society, it is vitally necessary to release these students from the Forces as soon as possible. They are indeed key-men in the repair and reconstruction of our society—one has only got to think of the impossibility of fulfilling the new Education Act without them to realise that. And yet in initiating a *Times* correspondence urging their release from the Forces, I received an anonymous, though quite literate, post-card from Ealing to say:

All arts students should be cleared out of the universities, to make way for science students.

We do not have to attach much serious importance to this expression of opinion in itself: it is obvious that the anonymous person from Ealing is a fool of the first water, much more of a fool than the famous Person from Porlock whose emergence upon the literary scene had such unfortunate consequences. But there is also no doubt that though this is an extreme, and indeed ridiculous, expression of opinion which no one need take seriously, it does represent, in its foolish way, something of a general bias in people's minds in favour of science as against the social sciences. They think that science is more "useful." They do not go further to reflect that the social sciences are even more useful, and more indispensably necessary if contemporary society is to solve the problems with which it is faced; that our really urgent problems are *not* in the realm of natural science at all—we are continually finding more than enough to go on with there (though I am all in favour of our going on), but that if we are not to destroy ourselves and civilisation we must build up the social and political organisations to bring these terrible forces under control and turn them into forces for the good of mankind; that in fact—as the whole of this book shows, or it shows nothing—the human sciences are in this age the most vital, the most essential and the most exciting objects of our intellectual effort.

And yet the half-baked, the half-educated Ealing Idiot can think of nothing more indispensable than that the students of social sciences should be cleared out of the universities. (Perhaps he does not know that the social sciences are the same thing as the arts.) If there is one thing the times we live in teach us it is that there is nothing more dangerous than the half-educated: all the really bad men from whom the world has suffered so much in our time come into this category, all the Hitlers and Mussolinis, the Ribbentrops, Cianos and Lavals—to go no further afield or to come no nearer home.

It is not only at the universities then that history has become the leading arts subject. I agree with Trevelyan's general judgment: "The older I get and the more I observe the tendencies and conditions of our latter day, the more certain I become that history must be the basis of humane (that is, non-scientific) education in the future. Without some knowledge of history other doors will remain locked. For example, the reading of poetry and prose literature, other than current books, must rest on some knowledge of the times past when the older books were written. Some understanding of the social and political scene of Chaucer's, Shakespeare's, Milton's, Swift's world, of the world of Boswell, of Wordsworth and Shelley and Byron, of Dickens and of Trollope, of Carlyle and Ruskin is necessary in order fully to appreciate the works in question, or even in some cases to understand what they are about. Music needs no such historic introduction to be fully appreciated, for it is not allusive, or only slightly. But literature is allusive, each book rooted in the soil of the time when it was written. Unless our great English literature is to become a sealed book to the English people (as indeed I fear it is to many) our countrymen must know something of times past."

That is already a very strong case; but I think

the case is stronger still. There is nothing that gives unity to all the other arts subjects so much as history. So many of them spring out of it, or find much of their material in history—such subjects as anthropology and sociology, economics and law, to a lesser extent languages. All of them have their historical aspect and meet together in history. It is a subject above all catholic, capacious, mixed; not a pure subject like mathematics, music or logic: it is as wide and various as life. Nor does it only provide the best common meeting-ground for all the separate arts disciplines; it gives them the best and most fruitful junction with the natural sciences.

Does this sound abstract and unreal? Do I need to illustrate what I am trying to say?

It should be quite simple. Suppose you are a student of a foreign language and literature, let us say French. You are bound to know something of the history of the people, if you are to understand their literature; and the development of the language will lead you back again to their history, which to some extent it reflects. If you are a student of anthropology or sociology or comparative law or ethics, you will derive much of your material from the history of different peoples, and without an historical sense, telling you where it comes in their development and what the circumstances are, you will not interpret it aright. The sociological circumstances of a given time and people will find expression in their literature; the dominant ethical code in their law and legislation. In each case the common ground is the history of that people and time, of which each shows a different aspect and to which they all contribute. The same holds good for the sciences and their relation to the arts. The development of science is intimately connected with the philosophical thought of its time no less than with its practical needs. Early astronomy developed in response to the demands of religious observance as well as the needs of travel by land and sea; navigation and commerce have given rise to much scientific discovery; geometry arose from the necessity for land-measurement. The student of geography will find that his subject goes hand in hand with geology on one side and history on the other. The study of geographical exploration is as much history as it is geography. Some of the classics of science are also classics of literature, for example, Bacon, Galileo, the works of Darwin and Huxley. Such arts as architecture and music have a scientific aspect; the story of their technical developments is a part of history. One can study the evolution of instruments: the pianoforte from the harpsichord and so from the virginals, the violin from the viol and the lute. And there is the whole historical approach to science itself; the men who made the achievements of science were men of their time, conditioned by the intellectual and social interests and character of their time. One recalls that the greatest statesman of Greek antiquity, Pericles, was a close friend of the great scientist Anaxagoras; the poet Euripides was another of his friends. In fact the cross-contacts and affiliations in the realm of knowledge are infinitely valuable and fertilising. But they all have their earth-bed in history, so to say, if this is not too passive a metaphor for a subject which operates more as a galvanic conductor, or a stream of connective energy in its own right.

From the time of the Renaissance up to our own time the Classics and the Bible occupied the centre of the field in humane studies and operated as the chief unifying influence in education. This was roughly true all over Europe (except for Russia and the Balkans), and it had a great effect in making a common European mind among the educated classes, in spite of national and religious divisions. Educated men had Plato and Aristotle, the Greek tragedians and historians, Virgil and Horace, Plutarch, Livy, Tacitus, the literature and history of the Bible, as a common background all over the Western world. It remained in full force in education in this country up to the last generation.

In the almost complete breakdown of the older classical education in our time all over Europe, where are we to look for a unifying influence to take its place? Where indeed but in history can our common experience and the different humane studies meet? I think there is no other possible

competitor, and this is the most important practical suggestion I have to make in this book.

It might be argued that history is a disunifying
influence rather than a unifying one; that nations
would be still further fortified in their own national
traditions and not look beyond their boundaries
to a European or a world community.

There can be no doubt of the immense stimulus
to courage and high endeavour that people derive
from knowledge of the great deeds of their past.
As I write, I have just read a remarkable article
by a young officer, Lieut. Norman Scarfe, in *The
Gunner*, the official paper of the Royal Artillery.
It is called "The Pen and the Sword" and its
theme is the inspiration that fighting men get from
the historic memories of their people's past at the
very moment of going into action. "An officer
of the Russian Artillery in the Crimean War," he
writes, "knew all about the value of the Regi-
mental Story. During pauses in the battle he
would sit with the men in their dug-out and re-
count the stirring episodes of their past in tribal
and frontier wars and in their victory over
Napoleon in 1812." (The artillery officer he is
thinking of, I suppose, must be Tolstoy.) He goes
on: "Another parallel I cannot at this point help
remarking in the 8th British Infantry Brigade,
which my regiment supported from 6th June,
1944, to 5th May, 1945, is the example of Major
C. K. ('Banger') King, D.S.O., who read aloud
to his men stirring historic passages from their

greatest poet, Shakespeare, as their assault
landing-craft approached the Calvados coast that
wild immortal morning."

I find that singularly touching. What did he
read to them, I wonder? Passages from *Henry V*, I
feel sure:

This day is called the feast of Crispian:
He that outlives this day and comes safe home . . .

The man who read to his men came home no
more: he was killed later on, before Bremen.
But he must have had another memory in his
mind: that still, grey shrouded night two hundred
years before on the St. Lawrence, and Wolfe
repeating Gray's Elegy to *his* men. (*What* a
tribute from a hero to a don!) But so men are
inspired to give all they have.

Something of the extraordinary emotional
appeal that the film *Henry V* had for us in this
country, coming as it did in the year of our invasion of Normandy, was due to the way in which
it struck such deep historic memories and brought
them back to us in the historic present when
every one of us held his breath for anxiety and
hope, love and grief. So too we know the
inspiration that the Russian people derived in
their trials from the great memory of 1812. And
no doubt our enemies found consolation and
comfort in recalling Frederick the Great's heroic
struggle against overwhelming odds.

It is perhaps true that the mental world of the

average man is that of his own country and its language and literature. But increasingly today, with newspapers, wireless and films, he is enabled to form some picture, if a partial and uneven one, of other countries. (Most English people have an infinitely better idea of America than of any other country, of the States three thousand miles away than they have of their next-door neighbour France.) But it is precisely in so far as people are educated that they become more aware and more capable of understanding other nations and their traditions. The man who has a good historical education is not confined to one country's view of its own past: the educated Englishman does not share George III's view of the American Revolution, any more than the educated American looks at it through the eyes of John Hancock or Sam Adams—or for that matter, of Colonel Mac-Cormick. As our historical reading widens and our judgment of events matures, we find great achievements and great mistakes and much humdrum endurance everywhere in the human record; and we come to see all the histories of different peoples, with their contacts of peace and war, their currents of mutual influence and reaction, their parallels and affiliations, their similarities and contrasts, all as part of one history. Arrived at that view-point, history is the most synoptic and unifying of all studies. But it implies, and demands, education; fortunately also it provides it. The process is a dual one.

One of the great advantages of history in education is that the subject grows with you from a very elementary stage to the last refinements of ripe maturity and sceptical wisdom. The subject is capable of appealing to quite young children, as I remember in my own case and have described in *A Cornish Childhood*: how a great-aunt of mine had a history book (there were no books in our house); it must have been a wonderfully dreary text-book of a very hot Protestant character, but I was fascinated by what it said about Mary Tudor and passionately enraged against her. This must have been at about the age of six. History is certainly capable of arousing the passions. This is no very dangerous thing, perhaps, at the age of six, and all to the good since it awakens interest. The sedate Dr. Keatinge in a useful little book, *Studies in the Teaching of History*, tells us: "It is as an introduction to the world of human nature that history is chiefly to be prized. If stress is laid on the biographical side, history is a panorama of character in action in every conceivable situation, it widens indefinitely the circle of our acquaintances, it provides abundant material for the analysis of motive, it gives opportunity for cultivating restraint in the admiration of pleasant personalities and charity in the judgment of unpleasant ones."

And that is about right. Children are very interested in personalities and their stories; they have a shrewd sense of character, which is developed by learning about persons in history and how they behave; after all it is only an extension of the living world they inhabit, with this added advantage—that they can see how things turned out with them: it gives them a basis for reflection. They do not inhabit a world of atoms and molecules, protons and electrons, chemical substances and atomic numbers—at least these do not form their personal acquaintance whom they have to learn to get on with in life. And though it may be said that the essential business of learning to get on with other human beings, to know them and understand them and judge their nature, is to be learned in the commerce of life itself, yet that same life portrayed pictorially, as it were, unrolled before our eyes in history, is a valuable extension of life and a great aid to our reflecting upon it. It is true, alas, that a great many people learn very little anyway; but that is no argument against what they might learn if they set themselves about it. And Dr. Keatinge states an extremely strong case for the study of history in schools even on purely utilitarian grounds:

"Most schools of any importance have a science laboratory, upon which a considerable sum of money is spent yearly; for the history lesson few schools supply any apparatus but a textbook and a blackboard. Natural science, as a branch of knowledge equipped with methods and apparatus, has had the start of social science. Moreover, it appeals to the crude utilitarian instinct and, in spite of the efforts of headmasters, who know their business, the pressure of pseudo-utilitarianism is one which it is difficult to resist."

After allowing that it is desirable that all schoolboys should be introduced to the world of science and to the elements of scientific method, Dr. Keatinge continues: "But once his schooldays are over, not one boy in a hundred will ever again be brought into contact with chemical processes or be compelled to make any physical calculations. The ordinary adult pays experts to perform these operations for him, and as a rule is too sensible to run the risk of doing them badly. . . . It is different with the other great department of school studies. The youth may never again see a test tube or a balance, but he cannot fail to be brought into contact with men. . . . His success in life will probably, will almost certainly, depend upon the ease and correctness with which he observes words, both written and spoken, and draws inferences from them; he will on countless occasions need to analyse documents, to abstract them, and to compare them; he will seldom be free from the necessity of inferring motives from actions and character from deeds; and it is precisely to these classes of mental operations, and to familiarity with these factors in human life, that school history, if properly conceived, and the history lesson, if properly conducted, will introduce him."

Surely everyone must agree with this out of his

own experience, if he reflects on it? It is not that I am against the teaching of science in schools; indeed I think it is important. But I also think there is too much of it, considering its general educational value. There is rather an unthinking bias in favour of science in schools nowadays; people assume that it must be the right thing, since 'This is a scientific age,' etc. and it leads obviously to certain careers in industry and elsewhere—but without reflecting whether it provides a general education for the mind. I note with interest that two enlightened and up-to-date science masters at Winchester, Messrs. Humby and James, in their book on *Science in the Schools* are inclined to doubt the value of chemistry as a school subject. Who am I to disagree with them? They know more about it than I do. I am not opposed to it in boys' schools, since I know that a good many boys learn through their hands rather than their heads. But I deeply doubt whether physics and chemistry have any educational value, save for a few exceptions, in girls' schools at all. I should have thought that in these their place might be more profitably taken, for obvious reasons, by biology, hygiene and natural history—sciences of life rather than of matter.

The expense of teaching history is inconsiderable compared with that of science, which demands more and more apparatus and laboratory equipment. The laboratory of history is the world we move about in. And it is desirable that teachers of history should be cultivated people capable of introducing their pupils to the diversity and richness, the memories and associations of the world immediately about them. Nothing of all that was done for me when I was at school; but then it was an inferior school and a quarter of a century ago. What can be done may be seen from a most useful little source-book compiled by the history masters at a Yorkshire school, Rothwell in the West Riding: it builds up a picture of the locality as it looked at different periods, from reliable historical sources, and thence to the wider region; in the end you see the history of the country depicted in the neighbourhood you know. Every school in the country that is any good ought to have a similar book—half-guide to the country, half-history—compiled for it.

Think of the delectable riches there are waiting to be opened up, and how fortunate we are in this country with so varied and fertile a soil to cultivate. At once there leaps to mind the thought of the castles of Wensleydale or the Vale of Pickering—with which Professor Powicke introduces us to *Medieval England*; the churches and manor-houses and small towns of the Cotswolds or East Anglia, the fortresses of the Welsh borders, the little sea-ports of the West Country. They all have their fascinating stories, the sediment of so many tides of life, the life of our forefathers, passing in and out of them. And what of the magnificent storied pageants of the past in the towns—Exeter, Bristol, Oxford, Norwich, Durham, York, London? They should all of them have their own source-books, the country's history as reflected in that mirror, as it actually happened in that place. An interesting job of work here, both of research and exposition, for history teachers in schools all over the country.

It should go hand in hand with regular planned expeditions, taking history classes to the interesting things in the neighbourhood, whatever they may be—barrows, stone-circles, camps, churches, castles, sites of battles, houses of interest, neighbouring villages and towns. You could get a very good idea of the chronological unfolding of the country's history from following some such order. One might even hope that as the idea spread in the country people would gradually cease to look at things of beauty with unseeing, uncaring eyes. One might even hope that they would cease to wreck and ruin the wonderful heritage the country got from the past, as against the infallible instinct of Philistinism for destroying what it cannot appreciate. We might even— shades of Matthew Arnold—cease to be Philistines! Nothing of this was ever undertaken at my school: one has had to learn its possibilities for oneself. But really, it need not be so: there is no end to the interest and fascination that can be got out of it.

Of course, all this goes along with books; but not only with books—with plays and films and wireless. They can all be brought into use and enjoyment—the twin themes of this book. Take plays, for example. It is wonderful how Shakespeare can always hold the interest of a class of schoolboys. I well remember my militant, mutinous dislike of Spenser's *Faerie Queene*—that exquisite dream-like poem, so wildly unsuitable as a set book for an examination. But not one of us disliked Shakespeare, or did not enjoy reading his plays in class; and, as has often been observed, by the most eminent of scholars as well as by the most refractory of schoolboys, there is a great deal of English history to be learned from Shakespeare's plays. Naturally, I am still more in favour of boys and girls acting them for themselves, and being taken to see productions of them whenever there is a chance.

The same holds good of films. Historical films, particularly American—for the Americans have little sense of history—have a long lee-way to make up. One of the things that gave me such satisfaction with the English film, *Henry V*, was to see a film at all that was not historically ridiculous. It was sheer pleasure to see the lovely, complex, coloured costumes of the late Middle Ages absolutely as they were, carefully studied from pictures and illuminated manuscripts; to hear the music that they actually sang, with its virile primitive harmonies; to see the buildings, the scenes, the ships, the accoutrements as they really were. I remembered, by way of contrast, how the Ameri-

can film, *Jane Eyre*, had been ruined for me by
the historical idiocy of Hollywood. As we all
remember from the book, the action takes place in
a plain, sober, substantial country-house of the
North Country, presumably Georgian in character. Not so in the film. Hollywood's idea of
an English country-house in the early nineteenth
century was donjons and battlements and corri-
dors like a bogus-Norman Tower of London.
Mr. Rochester, it will be remembered, enter-
tained a country-house party. They all came over
in a coach out of the romantic period of the
Wild West; but the lady who descended from it,
the *belle* of the party, was got up to look like one
of the *louche* ladies of the Restoration Court of
Charles II. It was all *pour rire*. It may be
regarded as a disadvantage to know too much
history, if it prevents one from enjoying such
nonsense. But surely it would be more fun to
get it right? And isn't it a pity that innocent
Americans should be given such fantastic ideas of
English country-house life?

As for the books, since history is one of the
cheapest subjects to teach, costing next to nothing
in equipment, schools should afford good history
books and pay for good teachers to teach the
subject. I think we can honestly say that there
has been an enormous improvement both in the
books and in the teaching of history all through
the country in our time. The older text-books—
which shall be nameless—used to be deadly,

guaranteed to kill any interest in the subject; the subject itself a Cinderella in most schools, and even at the universities. But all that has changed. Even as a small child one can begin with the most fascinating of books, like Eileen and Rhoda Power's *Boys and Girls of History* and *More Boys and Girls of History*; and from there go right on, with books that hold one's interest all the way along.

I think the royal road to appealing to the interest of the schoolboy, and not only the schoolboy, is the biographical: lives of great men, especially men of action, like the great English seamen or soldiers and adventurers and their exciting stories; and of course, secondly, if the two can be regarded separately, the stories themselves —the foundation of narrative history. Schoolboys respond immediately to the appeal of patriotism, to the spirit of self-devotion in such lives as Wolfe, Sir John Moore, Nelson, Livingstone, General Gordon, Scott of the Antarctic, Lawrence of Arabia. They feel the thrill of achievement in such careers as Clive's or Drake's or Rhodes'; they are capable of catching something of the greatness of spirit of such a man as Cromwell or Chatham, William Pitt or Winston Churchill. I am not so old as to have forgotten the spirit of emulation that is aroused in the schoolboy, the desire to make a name in his turn, to join the ranks of those who have achieved something by which their country remembers them. I think I might have responded even to science if it had been presented sympathetically, through history and biography. A shortened version of Darwin's *Voyage of the Beagle*, or his *Autobiography* or a life of him would have been the best introduction. No schoolboy could fail to respond to the life of Faraday. Even chemistry—of all things—might have gained some adventitious interest through the life of Sir Humphry Davy: that would have combined the appeal of a glamorous success-story with that of Cornish patriotism.

Fairly soon the schoolboy is capable of a psychological intuition that adults are apt to forget and overlook. (One should not forget that Elizabethan schoolboys were capable of the emotional range of playing Shakespeare's heroines, and remembering that one may understand a lot.) Quite soon a critical interest in character develops and is ripened by observing the mutual exchanges of Mary Tudor and Elizabeth, or of Elizabeth and Mary Stuart, the part played in our history by such harridans as Margaret of Anjou and Henrietta Maria, or by such incompetent, if pious, fools as Henry VI and James II. Dr. Keatinge quotes as an example of a document to study the remarkable letter Queen Elizabeth wrote to James of Scotland on the execution of his mother. It is an extraordinary psychological study; there is the whole complex situation written in brief in it: the sense of guilt, the Queen defending herself for what was an act of political necessity, a hateful dilemma imposed on her; in the same sentence asserting her innocence and yet that the step was justified; there is her anxiety at what James will do; a genuine regret mingled with relief that now it is all over; there is both sincerity and insincerity in it; ending up with propitiation and the hint of a bribe, the suggestion of common interest, that if James plays her game all will yet be well for him. *What* a document! *What* a woman! one feels as one reads it and reads it again. And yet I believe that almost any boy or girl would recognise the psychological subtlety of it and see the situation from the letter. (At the same time as one has a very low view of people's intellectual standards, one has a strong conviction that they could greatly improve on them if only they would try!)

The truth is that there is no subject that more demands judgment or develops it more naturally. And it is judgment of human beings and their affairs, of motives and causes of action and its effects, that history develops; with natural science, not: it is a technical judgment that is there developed.

The adolescent schoolboy of today, growing up into the contemporary world with its ubiquitous cynicism and its cheap disbeliefs, becomes very much alive—as people in general in the Victorian Age were not—to the gap between people's pretensions and their real motives, to the illusions they cherish, and—still more extraordinary— the way they hold on to them even when they know they are illusions, to the half-conscious game of double bluff that people play with themselves and with others. A schoolboy, from the oldest of English schools, had something of this in his mind when he asked me quite recently whether the study of history did not make one completely sceptical. The answer is that it does make one salutarily sceptical of pretensions, and the larger and more high-sounding they are the more one has to beware—one is so used to that kind of thing in history, one has so often been there before. One develops a preternaturally keen scent for humbug in all its forms: one knows that what people put forward as the universally good is almost always something that suits their own interests. It is probably the moralist that is the easiest prey to humbug: it is so very near to his usual stock-in-trade. The historian is hardly ever to be caught out this way: he has seen it at work too often in too many climes at too many times. Of course, he has his own dangers: he is apt to be bored by human silliness in so many different forms and guises, to throw up the sponge and say nothing can be done with human beings or for them, that they are unteachable and irredeemable (as they often seem to be), that the truth about human affairs is that

Tout passe, tout casse, tout lasse.

In short the historian's danger *is* scepticism, indifferentism; his temptation, despair.

And yet it is perhaps significant that though all historians have some scepticism, and some have been morally indifferent, not one has really despaired—as some of the greatest of writers have despaired. Not even Hume or Gibbon, or Voltaire, or for that matter Machiavelli. The answer to the intelligent schoolboy is that if there is much folly in the human record, there is also much greatness; if there is great insincerity and hypocrisy and selfishness there is even more sincerity, single-mindedness, goodness of heart— and these are to be found everywhere, though never more notably than among the greatest and most gifted of men. As against man's cruelty one must fairly place his infinite capacity for self-sacrifice. One can go even further and say that on the whole history shows—as life does, but history proves it—that it is better to be honest and true than to be bad, however clever one may be. Even Mr. Chamberlain was against Hitler in the end—and he was stupid enough in all conscience, but honest. The Hitlers and William Rufuses and Richard III's are apt to come to sticky ends. And though in human affairs innocence is sometimes betrayed and goodness defeated, the balance shown by history as on a chart—and nowhere else can you see it—is indubitably the other way. It really does pay to tell the truth and stick to it, to be courageous (without being foolhardy), to work hard and do one's duty, to love well and truly. That schoolboy's question brings us up against

178

the difficult intellectual issues treated in the last chapter; well aware of them as I am and of their corrosive influence upon the modern mind, I think I can reply simply that the effect of studying history is to make one a realist, possibly a little pessimist (according to temperament)—but never a cynic. In short, in old-fashioned language, history is a school of virtue.

These things apply with still more force at the university stage of education, for it is then that the ratiocinative, the reflective faculties come more fully into play and young men develop the quality of intellectual judgment. Nothing surprises me more, or affords more ground for hope, than the way in which intelligent schoolboys of today already display these qualities: to a remarkable extent—far more, I am sure, than in my time at school. What is it that the study of history at the university can do for one in this regard?

Perhaps I may be allowed to refer to my own personal experience: it may serve to bring the point home. When I was at school my attitude to history—as to everything else—was emotional and passionate: it was an affair of prejudices, of sympathies and repugnances. For example, my emotions were passionately on the side of King and Church in the Civil War: I could not bear their defeat. I now recognise, though my likes and dislikes remain the same, that it was good for the country that Parliament won and the Cavaliers were defeated. That was the right way through to the future. My emotional preferences were, and are, Catholic—certainly not Protestant; but I have no doubt now that the Protestant Reformation was the making of the good fortune of this country. So far from regretting it—and there were regrettable sides to it, notably the destruction of the monasteries and the dispersal of their treasures—yet we cannot be grateful enough to the (sometimes unattractive) Henricians and Elizabethans who pushed us through it.

Of course there are plenty of historians who allow their emotional prejudices to bedevil their judgment. Their reason is at the service of their emotions; their emotions mould their reason. Take Belloc and Chesterton as examples, those two big bouncing boys of prejudice, who have had such a deplorable influence in rewriting our history and making nonsense of it. With them it is only too obvious. But it is no less obvious, to anyone who understands a little psychology, with a much subtler and more brilliant mind, Newman. If you read his novel *Loss and Gain*—which is very revealing of himself—you will see how all his sympathies at school were with King and Church. He never got over them. The whole of his subsequent mental history was a subtle process of finding intellectual reasons to prove what his heart had long ago opted for. I call that very feminine: I understand the process well.

Le cœur a ses raisons, it has been said; and it may

be thought an uncomfortable state of affairs to have the reasons of the heart on one side and those of the mind on the other. But is one to prefer one's own comfort to honesty and not being afraid to look things straight in the face and seeing them for what they are? I regard the latter choice as altogether more intellectually adult, more mature.

I am convinced that I owe the development of my reason to going to the university: one of the greatest among all the good things in life that I owe to Oxford. One may say, giving me the benefit of the doubt, that some rational development would have come about in any case; that it was only a question of growing older. But it would not have been the same. Before I went up to the university I was incapable of defending logically, or even of expounding clearly and in orderly fashion, what it was that I thought, or rather felt. As the result of living constantly in the world of discourse of the intelligent undergraduate, of endless discussions and arguments, in the end there was no kind of position that I did not feel capable of defending, no case that one could not at least state. Perhaps that is an exaggeration; but a pardonable one, that makes my argument clear.

What part did the study of history play in all this? What has it to offer to the mind's development at the university? What are the faculties that it elicits and strengthens? What are its effects?

Of course it does not cover the whole ground

of a young man's mental development, any more than any other special discipline does, languages or one of the sciences or philosophy. But though in itself it only covers a part of the ground, it is wider, more general and diverse than any other specialisation. That already gives a clue to the kind of mind that it appeals to and the quality of mind that it brings out. History is not a subject for your narrow, niggling, precise mind: let him take to logic or economics. It needs rather a capacious and generous mind: there is an awful lot to take in—no end to it, in fact—and it demands a great deal of reading. It has rather the advantage that attaches to Bacon's "Reading maketh a full man." He goes on to say that writing makes an 'exact' man. History is not without its advantages from this point of view too. It sets a premium on accuracy, on adherence to fact. It is no use having a general impression that the battle of Waterloo took place somewhere or other, or at another time than it did. I think the thing that impresses me most about my colleagues who are historians is their accuracy of mind, accuracy to fact and circumstance. Lawyers have an even greater and more precise accuracy: a greater verbal exactness. And for a combination of subtlety with precision you have to look to the philosophers or logicians, or to the mathematicians—but they do not speak the language of common humanity. The study of history gives you a common-sense accuracy, rather than a subtle precision; even more, it demands capacity.

It is also, as we have already seen, a science of judgment. It is all the time concerned with human beings and their affairs, public and private, social and individual; so that even at school it elicits judgment of human conduct, for it is an extension of our common-sense experience of it. (History is, then, a great school of common sense.) At the university a further, rather subtler development of judgment comes into play. History rests on documents of various kinds—landscape, buildings, monuments, books, papers, deeds, letters, inscriptions, scraps, sherds; and the teaching of history at the university is much concerned—it might be more—with the interpretation of documents. This introduces a subtlety well defined by Dr. Keatinge: "In history, as opposed to natural science, the fact which is at hand for observation is not the historical fact, but merely a description of it, and in many, if not in most cases, a very unreliable one. The transition from the document to the fact is difficult, occupies a great part of the historian's time, and dictates to him the nature of his method. In history there is thus an additional, and frequently a very uncertain step, which is not to be found to the same extent in natural science." It is therefore that Seignobos tells us that "all historical knowledge being indirect, history is essentially a science of reasoning."

It is on account of the *general* character of the subject, its essential concern with human affairs, that Bacon is enabled to say that where the poets make man "witty; the mathematics, subtle; natural philosophy, deep; moral, grave; logic and rhetoric, able to contend . . . histories make men wise."

Though it does not compete with philosophy on its own ground, the study of history is not without some abstract value. As we have seen, it opens up severe intellectual problems of its own, problems that have a great deal more importance for us than many of the metaphysical problems that have consumed so much time and attention in the past. As an undergraduate studying history at Oxford my mind became increasingly possessed by the problems discussed in the last chapter, the issues of historical relativism and scepticism, the doctrines of, and questions raised by, Marxism. And whatever may be thought of the conclusions I came to, there can be no doubt of the part these difficulties and the struggle to solve them played in my intellectual development. I should never have obtained such grasp as I have of them if I had not been soused up to the neck in them—sometimes, even in danger of going under. Perhaps I may be allowed to contrast a contemporary at Oxford, the Communist writer, Ralph Fox. He never ceased to regret to me that he had not read history, instead of languages. It meant for him that he had not an intellectual line of his own on these questions that have been so crucial for our generation. For want of it, he followed the "Party-line": it sent him to a nameless grave in Spain, along with other good Englishmen superfluously sacrificed to an alien orthodoxy.

But, indeed, the study of history leads straight to an intense, and responsible, concern with politics. The whole of this book proves why: politics is the continuation of history in our time, it is history being made under our eyes. One is impelled therefore by the very nature of one's studies to take a closer interest in public affairs. If one's subject is the dissection of frogs, or the beauties of number, one's impulse toward politics is (I fancy) less strong. At the same time, the fact that one's study is history gives one an altogether better basis for political judgment; most people's political judgment is silly or inadequate for want of such a basis. I can only say that I should never have been so interested in politics if my tutors at Oxford had not taken me away from English Literature, in which I had won a scholarship, and made me read history. There can be no doubt that the great increase of interest in politics among students at the universities since the last war has gone hand in hand with the immense development of the History Schools in them. At the beginning of this century Professor A. F. Pollard could lament that modern history was the Cinderella of London University, and certainly he cites an incredibly small number of students. Gone are those days: he himself changed all that at London University, which must now have one of the largest history faculties in the country. At Oxford the School of Modern History is the largest of all the Schools, and in addition there are the ancient historians who form part of the Greats faculty. It is, I hope, not invidious to say that the Oxford School is the leading historical school in the country, not only by reason of its size and output, but by the indubitable fact that the history faculties of so many other universities at home and in the Empire—not to mention the United States—are fed from it.

It is interesting to note how many of the younger generation of politicians in the new House of Commons, elected in 1945, have graduated from History and Modern Greats, and politically through the University Labour Club, at Oxford. During the last twenty years in my experience the association has been very close; and I have shown that there is a reason for it. Two generations ago they would have come from the Greats School— classics and ancient history—as Asquith and Grey did, Morley and Bryce, Curzon and Lang, and many others, like Sir Robert Morant, whose names are not so well known but who have left their mark on our history. If I may make a criticism of that school for which, like all Oxford men, I have the deepest respect, I have noticed it as a great disadvantage among its products that they should know the history of Greece and Rome so well, and of their own country and modern Europe hardly at all. Anyhow, better any history than none.

It is remarkable too how many of the contemporary generation of writers have come from the History School at Oxford: Guedalla, Arthur Bryant, Michael Sadleir, Aldous Huxley; Cyril Connolly, Evelyn Waugh, Graham Greene; David Cecil, C. V. Wedgwood. It is a matter of melancholy pride that the two most distinguished war-poets of this war, Alun Lewis and Sidney Keyes, were both historians, where their predecessors of the last war, Rupert Brooke and Wilfred Owen, were classics and linguists.

A word about the organisation of the School that occupies such a central place in university education may be useful. It is dominated by the Final Examination to which reading and teaching are directed over a course of three years. There are three papers that cover the whole of English history, dividing it up into three periods. In my time there were separate papers on political, constitutional and economic history. I regard it as a great improvement that those divisions were abolished—an improvement with which the argument of this book is wholly in line. For it is ultimately much less valuable to read political history divorced from constitutional, and constitutional divorced from economic. It is more exciting intellectually, if more difficult, to see how these things act and react upon one another; it is more fertilising to the life of the mind to grasp them in association with each other, and in any case closer to the truth of things and the way they happen. The most fascinating questions, regarded academically, are often borderline questions: they tended to be left out formerly; not so now. There is a fourth paper on the constitutional documents of English history, either medieval or modern with passages from set books and statutes. Altogether you have the background of English history, the core of the School. Plenty of scope for the widest capacity and reflection— one can never cover it all equally or read enough to please oneself, though one may please the examiners. The documents are a test of accuracy, attention to detail, ability to interpret—besides the light they throw on the history.

Next, there are two papers on a selected period of foreign history, usually covering something like a century. You may choose almost any period you like; the most popular is the nineteenth century, the stretch of history beginning with the French Revolution. And that is quite right on Bury's principle that modern history is the most important to study. At the same time one doesn't want everybody studying the same period; and it is a good thing that the next most popular stretch is the sixteenth century, that of Renaissance and Reformation out of which modern Europe (except Russia and the Balkans) emerges. Then there is a special subject, which must be taken by those who aspire to a good class: a wide range of historical subjects from which to choose, from St. Augustine to modern Labour Movements. Two papers are set, one of which is given up to the documents and original authorities for the subject. The purpose of this is obvious: a more searching test of accuracy, attention to detail, and of the interpretation and use of evidence.

There are two general papers, more abstract in character. One in political theory, which is based on the study of Aristotle's *Politics*, Hobbes' *Leviathan* and Rousseau's *Contrat Social* as texts and on the history of modern political theory; the other dealing with general questions of historical method and research, the intellectual issues that arise in connection with history, aspects of the history of culture, of art and historical literature. This is a new paper since my time as an undergraduate, and one that goes to fill a need which I felt most acutely as a young student. There was far too little opportunity for this kind of general discussion of the issues raised by one's subject, especially as compared with Greats for example: one reason for the undoubted superiority of Greats over Modern History as a School at that time— and perhaps still. It will be seen that the weakness of the History School, as compared with Greats (Ancient History and Philosophy) and Modern Greats (Philosophy, Politics and Economics), is on the abstract side. Things have the defects of their qualities. These two papers do something to rectify the balance, which necessarily in history is on the side of fact and *was eigentlich gescheht*. Lastly there is a paper of translation from foreign languages: the student of modern history is expected to know two, Latin and one modern language.

Such is the structure of the Final Honours School of Modern History to which reading and teaching are directed at Oxford. It determines the plan of a student's work during his three years' course —he reads towards the end of that examination; though in the life of a residential university there is time for a good deal of reading outside his work. It is even more important, and more to the real purpose of a university, that he should become a cultivated man than that he should get a good class in the Schools. I recommend both.

It is not my purpose to describe the whole organisation of historical study at Oxford— professors, readers, lecturers, tutors; libraries, societies, clubs; writing and research. That would demand a book in itself. My object has simply been to provide an illustration of the use of history in educating the young student at a university and how it works.

So much then for history in education at school and university—though so much more might be said. Now to wider fields.

Chapter Seven

History and Culture:
Further Uses and Pleasures

HISTORY is an essential part of the mind of a cultivated man. One may be a cultivated man without knowing mathematics or chemistry or engineering, for those are specialisms. We expect the technicians in question to know them and to do our sums and sanitation for us. But some knowledge of history, or even more a sense of history, is, as we have seen, part of the self-awareness of our environment. In nothing is the degree of cultivation of a man more subtly revealed.

An uneducated man has no sense of history. He does not know whether the house he sees is Victorian or Georgian, Elizabethan or medieval; or what that means if told. He cannot tell whether it is beautiful or not: he has no means of judging, no sense of standards—for that, as Plato would say, is part of the same subject. Travelling up to the North Country the other day with a friend who is an historian, we were commenting on the buildings that caught our attention as we passed through strange towns. A friendly soldier

191

in the same compartment was astonished that we could tell at a glance roughly the dates when many of them were built. Yet there is nothing remote or difficult about that: anyone would have thought that we had achieved the differential calculus; whereas in fact it is open to anybody to get the hang of the building styles of different periods quite easily. And think of the interest it adds to knocking about the country! Most people go about the country with their eyes closed. It is from their ignorance and insensibility that the progressive ruin of the countryside, the wrecking of our old towns—they had the most beautiful urban architecture in the world—the hideousness of much of the new arises. (Can it be wondered at that I hate ignorance and stupidity more than anything else in the world?)

How well I remember from earlier days car-rides about the country with the uneducated: nothing more exquisitely agonising; no perception of the difference between this and that, between this that was beautiful—in fact, that they didn't like—and something else that was appalling; people who thought the place 'finely improved' when it had been thoroughly disfigured by a row of mean bungalows on the Cornish cliffs. The great majority of people belong to that category. But that does not mean that there are no standards, or that there is any doubt about them. The standards are quite well known to those who know; those who don't, do not know them; standards are in truth set by those who know, as they always have been. They are historically based; they spring out of long tradition, though the test of their value is an æsthetic one.

What is the purpose in my saying this? What good aim may be served by it? *To help as many people as possible to share in the mental life of civilised, cultivated people.* The world is astray, not because people are wicked or irremediably stained with some original sin, but for lack of cultivation, intelligence, reason, sense. I am going to be quite blunt, in the interests of my aim, and say what educated people really think about the uneducated. Hardly anybody ever dares to; there is a curious conspiracy not to, though we hear more than enough in contemporary literature of what uneducated people think of the educated. The loss is on the side of the uneducated: it is really not fair to them. I propose to reverse matters and to tell the truth.

There is nothing more boring for educated people in the society of the uneducated than the restriction of their conversation, the limitation of their mental world. Their horizon is restricted to the parish, in the country; in the towns, to the radius of the local cinemas; their sense of what is going on is crude and irrational; they have no means of judging or appraising events, of which, in consequence, they are victims. And there is nothing to talk to them about—except perhaps sex. (I know, for I have attempted the difficult experiment of continuing to live in touch with an original social environment on a lower level than my interests of mind; most people, on growing out of it, have done with it. There are some advantages to be gained from the point of view of social observation, to set against the acute discomforts, mainly of an æsthetic character.)

But no good purpose is served by our being defeatist. Far too many intelligent people are too diffident and give the case away to the Philistines and barbarians. Quite unnecessarily and unfairly; it is perhaps most of all unfair to the low-brows, who never arrive at the point of knowing what it is that keeps these others so interested and lively and releases them from being the preys of boredom.

The simple truth is that it is endlessly interesting and fascinating to have a mental life. For one thing, you are much less at the mercy of external circumstances. There is no end to the voyaging and explorations you can do. During the war it has been impossible for a great many people to travel, in space; but it has been all the more delightful to voyage in time, and, for that matter, in space too. It is that that accounts for the great growth of historical reading during the war and the long winters of black-out. A businessman of my acquaintance told me that for the first time he had taken up reading, mainly history, during the war, and of the extraordinary difference it had made to life, both for him and his

wife: the opening out of new horizons of illimitable interest, the widening of perspective in which
to view what happens around us—altogether something approaching in its effect to a conversion.

I know from experience in Cornwall what
interest uneducated people get from the lectures,
excursions and readings of Old Cornwall Societies.
In fact they get the beginnings of education from
them: they learn to *see* things, old places and
buildings, churches and holy-wells, castles and
camps, stone-circles and crosses, the evidences
and survivals of times past. They begin to get a
grasp of what the life of communities has been, of
which they are a part; they develop a sense of its
continuity; they become proud of their heritage.
Who can deny that that is a good thing, however
unfinished and crude it may be? And how
infinitely better than the appalling vacuity,
without savour or sense, coarse and adrift,
deriving the character of its ideas from Hollywood, its standards of behaviour from bar and
street-corner, of the bulk of the illiterate. It is
strictly true that the great majority of people see
nothing, hear nothing, understand nothing and
know nothing. I mean nothing much to speak
of—that is worth anything. *There* is the real
tragedy of the world. But it is perhaps reme-
diable. We can all do something to make ourselves less unintelligent than we are. It will be
seen that I am very far from being a cynic, but
that I am a (qualified) optimist.

It is all very well to turn your back on the things of the mind when you are young and active and can swim and cycle and run and ride and make love to the girls. All very well in their place, and I am entirely in favour. This don is no kill-joy, but the reverse. I am all in favour of enjoyment: that is part of my gospel. But the things of the mind and of the spirit are to be enjoyed too. Let us have no inhibitions on either side. It is bad to inhibit the life of the body; it is also bad to inhibit the life of the mind. The low-brows are just as wrong as the kill-joys. What one needs is to strike a balance, to achieve a due harmony so that the one can refresh and enliven the other.

It follows that in the days of your youth and health and strength you need to take some interest in the things of the mind, even if you are not naturally inclined to; for as you get older and physical resources fail you, you need something to fall back on. Actually one's interest in the things of the mind, once it has got root or is released, deepens and becomes riper as one grows older. And so with history. Our appreciation and understanding of it, our feeling for its subtleties and excitements grows with us as we get older, instead of failing us. As we grow less good at mounting the hills, we get better at seeing the place of Christianity in the development of our civilisation, at understanding what we owe to it and what it did for us, in civilising the barbarian peoples;

196

at appreciating the incomparable miracle that was Greece; at seeing Italy and France, from which we have derived so much, with discernment; at watching with loving interest the unfolding of the picture of life.

There is something pathetically childish about the uncultivated man. Not to have a sense of time is like having no ear or sense of beauty—it is to be bereft of a very exquisite faculty. It reminds me of a child I heard the other day, standing before a case of exhibits of the Elizabethan Age in the Victoria and Albert Museum and asking "Were you born then, Mummy?" But she was about seven or eight. The time-sense of most uneducated people is equally astray, quite childish: they are not adult.

Even educated people lose a lot of the subtlety in understanding things through not looking at them historically. I never cease to be taken aback by people's short-term judgments of nations and peoples—of the English, for example—on the basis of what they look like now. You cannot tell what a people really are until you see them in a long-term perspective. It is like expecting to know a man from one moment's look at him. And nations are very much more complex.

No wonder people abroad were surprised by Britain's resistance in 1940. They need not have been, if only they had read our history. It was in our whole history and tradition to resist: we always had resisted in similar disasters and come through. Or take America and the stupid conviction of the Germans that the Americans—because they were devoted to peace—were no fighters. Anyone knowing anything of American history knows that the Civil War was one of the toughest and hardest-fought wars in history, and look how they fought against us in the War of Independence. We had learnt from that; nobody made any mistake about it in this country, either in the last war or this.

People who do not know their history are liable to be fooled. I do not know whether to call not being fooled a use or a pleasure—it has the elements of both. But indeed we can now see that the dictators were really too ignorant. There is nothing more dangerous than to be ignorant.

M. Maillaud in an interesting book *The English Way* tells us what the Continental view of the English is. "The picture conjured up by the fairly well-educated Continental world presents the English as sporting, practical, sparing of words, business-like, conservative, disciplined, either puritanical or oddly eccentric and melancholy." That is a picture based on one reading of the Victorian age—even so, thoroughly inadequate. Nobody can think of the Victorian Englishman as 'sparing of words,' the age of Dickens, Carlyle, Gladstone, Spurgeon, General Booth—all those orators on platform or in pulpit. Nor was the earlier Englishman of the Elizabethan Age, or the eighteenth century, either, 'sparing of words' or

198

'puritanical,' 'disciplined' or 'melancholy.' There was always a genial, jovial quality about English social life, and continentals of earlier centuries thought of us as the most indisciplined of peoples.[1] It was a great mistake on the part of the dictators to think that the mood of appeasement betokened the decadence of the English people; underneath there were the old long-tried qualities patient and strong; held in restraint, but still there under the surface, was the old truculence that had refused to yield to so many tyrants, and seen them out.

It is most important for a nation to have a rational and common-sense, a true tradition of its own history: one that makes sense of the past and makes events and their upshot intelligible. It is an essential factor in the strength and coherence of a people and a chief element in their success and effectiveness. In the end, a false historical tradition is a terrible source of weakness and intellectual disarray, even though in the short run it promises to give a people greater cohesion, and pride in their past, and hence operate as a stimulus to action. Nations can be over-stimulated to disaster by short-term readings of their past. Neither Hitler nor Mussolini had any real sense of history, though each was cheaply and egotistically excited by melodramatic readings of history. The dream of modern Italy as an imperial power, the Mediterranean as ' *mare nostrum* ' and the rest of it, was indeed a nostrum that

[1] Cf. my book *The English Spirit*, pp. 23–4.

cost Italy thousands of lives and millions of money, and ended in nothing but wreckage, impoverishment and humiliation.

The influence upon Germans of a false reading of history has been even more tragic, for Germans are sure to believe the nonsense in which they wallow. Even now after the nightmare experience they have brought upon themselves and the world, by their pursuit of the dream of world-power as the logical end of the process of German history, they have still not learnt the essential lesson. Karl Barth tells us that "the real discussion has not started so long as one talks to the Germans only about Hitler. The crucial point is reached when the discussion comes to Bismarck. When the Nazi plaster has fallen away in dust there is revealed in the majority of Germans, even in those who have been active in opposition, the solid brickwork of German nationalism. They regard Nazism as a regrettable incident, but all before it is beyond criticism. They do not understand that Nazism was nothing else than the final outcome of the Bismarckian policy, which forged Germany with blood and iron into a National Socialist, capitalist, imperialist Reich, and so into the grave-digger of the vital freedom of 1848." *Was für ein Volk!* The Germans are the real Bourbons of modern history: they forget nothing except their own crimes, but neither do they learn anything.

Nothing could be more important for them than that they should understand the real significance of the career of Bismarck (or for that matter, of Luther) : how Bismarck's determination to eliminate liberalism, constitutional government, any form of democracy, stunted and eventually withered the development of responsible self-government in the German people; how his unification of Germany by force, the concentration upon military power, reduced European politics to those terms, and eventually produced a reply to the challenge that power was to the security of everybody else. It was Bismarck more than anybody who set Germany's feet upon the wrong path; and yet Germans for the most part have no conception of it.

The English have been willing to learn from the mistakes they made in the past. I think they have learned that there is no government like self-government. They made great mistakes in relation to Ireland in the past—not that the fault was all on one side, or that all the mistakes were avoidable: some of them were in the nature of things. But in our own time they have learned to leave Ireland alone to work out her own salvation in her own way. The moral is being drawn now in relation to India. A conscious attempt was made in imperial policy in the nineteenth century to avoid the mistakes made in the treatment of the American Colonies: hence the unexpected success, on the whole, of our record with Canada and the wonderful reward the Canadians have given us in this century of our peril.

Above all, we learned from the disruption of government and society in the Civil War of the seventeenth century, or rather, our governing class learned, and handed down what they had learnt to become the operative tradition of our policy, shared in progressively by all. (It is one of the most encouraging things in our time to observe the newest comer to power, the working-class movement, sharing in that tradition, exemplifying as well as any its moderation, restraint, its inherent sense of responsibility.)

Professor Butterfield tells us, in a most interesting essay, *The Englishman and his History*, that the Whig interpretation of our past has been a formative element in this. "The common law and the Whig interpretation have worked together to tighten the bonds that hold the Englishman to his past—have helped to foster our love of precedent, our affection for tradition, our desire for gradualness in change, our adherence to ancient liberties." In our own time we have seen this Whig view, with its emphasis on individual liberty, moderation and common sense, absorb what might have been a Tory alternative, the epic story of British expansion overseas. "Perhaps only in the shock of 1940," he says, "did we realise to what a degree the British Empire had become an organisation for the purpose of liberty. What power is in this English tradition which swallows up monarchy, toryism, imperialism, yet leaves each of them still existing, each part of a wider synthesis." I would only add that the greatest part of that epic story of the expansion of our stock is concerned with America; the United States are not outside the tradition: they are its greatest vindication— of the Whigs in particular. They are not anything different in kind: they are part of our very marrow.

The Professor goes on to analyse what is at the core of this political sense. He says that a recognisable element is "the feeling that, apart from any action we may take in some present conjuncture, the world is changing: and history is moving forward on her own account, and we ourselves must reckon with this process and use it—must conceive of ourselves as co-operating with history, leaning on events somewhat; not resting idly indeed, but lying in wait for opportunity." He concludes that "amongst all political crimes the attempt to fly in the face of history is the one that has suffered the heaviest retribution in the modern world." He contrasts "that tempered faith in the course of history" which is at the heart of the English tradition with the revolutionary course of some Continental countries: "It is not clear that Continental countries, which have had their revolutions, followed by counter-revolutions, have greatly improved on the English rate of progress, in spite of what they paid in havoc and bloodshed precisely for the sake of speed."

In France the Revolution created a great barrier, and still you are either on one side or on the other. It has impeded a unified conception of the past for the French, one making the history of France as a whole consistent and intelligible, doing justice to the work of both sides of that great divide. As it is, French history is written too much in partisan terms, either through royalist monocles or republican pince-nez. The interesting minds are those that escape these limitations. As an example of royalist myopia carried to ridiculous lengths, we may take the case of the history text-book on which the little Comte de Chambord, the legitimist heir to the throne, was brought up: which described the creative, the epic period from 1789 to 1815 in the words, "During these years the country was a prey to internal disruption." It is not surprising that that boy grew up into the political idiot who muffed his chances of the throne in the eighteen-seventies.

With this we reach the borderland between public use and private pleasures. Let us turn to the pleasures of conversation.

Since history is an extension, and a verification, of our experience it makes what is in itself a realm of delightful discourse one of great value. I must take leave to say that as a subject of conversation, compared with the weather, or bridge, or the dogs, it has greater variety and more intrinsic interest. It offers all the possibilities of what is admittedly the greatest subject of conversation among Englishmen—politics.

To share my own experience with you: I find it

one of the greatest pleasures of life, lasting and satisfying, if sober and sedate, to enjoy the conversation of friends of mine who are historians. The friend to whom I have dedicated this book is a medievalist, an authority on the fifteenth century, the period immediately preceding my special sphere of interest. We are in the habit of walking about the sweet Oxfordshire countryside to see villages, houses, churches or what you will, wherever it may be. The whole country comes alive for us in conversation, is peopled once more by the folk who lived their lives in these places and made a great figur 1 here centuries ago. As often as not they turn up in the churches, at Stanton Harcourt or Minster Lovell, Swinbrook or Asthall or Burford; at Bibury, Ablington, Winson or Colne Rogers; at Compton Beauchamp, Ashbury, Ashdown or Uffington; at Cricklade or Lechlade, Ampney Crucis or Fairford; Wallingford or Bensington or Ewelme, where Chaucer's granddaughter, the Duchess, lies in her state.

While we walk we talk: no lack of things to talk about: nothing of that horrid vacuity which is the penalty of being uncultivated. Another historian friend of mine, with whom I walk, knows about the seventeenth century. What more natural than to ask him questions about the people whom I know about in the sixteenth century and what has happened to them and their families? Such conversation offers the pleasure of gossip—I do not under-rate those pleasures—with none of the penalties. Other friends of mine give me tit-bits of information about the eighteenth century or are open to being questioned about the great issues of policy in debate then and that have affected us in so many ways since. How to describe the charm of a society like All Souls, where there is a body of men to whom, taken together, no period is alien? I can only repeat what a political friend of mine has said—that he does not bother to look up the encyclopædia: he knows that when he comes down into the common-room there will be bound to be somebody who can answer his question. We may not all be able to inhabit an All Souls; but we can all of us read and find friends of like interests.

I should be misleading you if I allowed you to suppose that these pleasures of conversation were merely the pleasures of gossip. There is poetry in them; behind it all, that sense of the underside of life, the brevity of our own lives, the continuity of all life and its pathos: all that hardly expressed, though it is there all the time like the sounds and scents of the countryside we are passing through, the music of a stream by the wayside (as it might be Eamont or Fal or Windrush), the steady noise of the wind in the trees like the sound of the sea, or dappled light and shadow brushing the blue bells of campanulas that spread over the banks of Grimsdyke. There is all the latent appeal to the imagination, hardly talked of, yet understood between us. A young soldier away at the war wrote me: "I acknowledge, gladly and proudly, that you and I share very fully the pleasures of appreciating music and literature; our countryside, too, architecture and art. But I wonder if you know how sour for me are the grapes of history, whose study, based as it is on years of intellectual effort more intense than I am capable of, yields you more solid joys, more lasting *pleasure*." But not so: that young soldier only lacks opportunity because of the years at the war; anybody capable of writing like that will have no difficulty in entering into the kingdom. This whole book is an answer to his *cri de cœur*, will show him how.

On a more prosaic level, there is so much to discuss, the fascinating patterns of motive, the intricacies of character, the astonishing stories that some people's lives make, the detective-thriller interest in tracking them down and where they lived, the ghosts.

A great deal of history may be learned, in the most congenial way, by reading biographies. We all know what Carlyle thought: "Social life is the aggregate of all the individual men's lives who constitute society; History is the essence of innumerable biographies." And again, on the lives of great men: "As I take it, Universal History, the history of what man has accomplished in this world, is at bottom the History of the Great Men who have worked here. They were the leaders of men, these great ones: the modellers, patterns, and in a wide sense creators, of whatsoever the general mass of men contrived to do or to attain; all things that we see standing accomplished in the world are properly the outer material result, the practical realisation and embodiment, of thoughts that dwelt in the Great Men sent into the world." Without going all the way with Carlyle in this, we can agree with the more limited proposition he goes on to: "One comfort is, that Great Men, taken up in any way, are profitable company. We cannot look, however imperfectly, upon a great man, without gaining something by him."

That is enough for our purposes; it follows that reading biographies is of value in itself. A first-rate biography will lead you straight into the atmosphere, the thoughts, will give you the very pulse, of the period. Many classical scholars would agree that Plutarch's *Lives* form the best introduction to Ancient Greece and Rome. Or take the greatest of English biographies, Boswell's *Life of Johnson*. It is a wonderful picture of an age and a society, that very remarkable society of which Dr. Johnson was the centre and easily the dominating figure. You hear them talking, you overhear what they thought about each other; more subtly, you can sense the atmosphere, the standards and values, the conventions and pre-judices, of the time. Then there are the characters, more varied, more convincing than any novel, and of far more remarkable people: there is genial, good-natured, equable Sir Joshua; shy, touchy, timid Goldsmith, constant target for the Doctor's sallies; affectionate, irresistible David Garrick, vain as any actor must be, whose relations with Johnson, though intimate, were difficult, for the younger Garrick had early and easily found the success that came so late and with so much reluctance to Johnson; the sly, conceited, affected Gibbon with his precise manner, who said nothing in that company but took in everything. And then the great Johnson himself: how to describe him? Impossible: one can but go to Boswell. I will say one thing only of Johnson: he is the nearest thing the English have ever produced to a Socrates.

Or what a portrait of the Victorian age we have through a leading figure, and a very central one in intellectual society, in Froude's *Life of Carlyle*. Good critics think this the first of our modern biographies: it certainly marked a change from the conventional Victorian biography in the critical candour of its treatment of the subject. All the more admirable considering Froude's veneration of Carlyle. There was an outcry at Froude's failure to treat the subject with the usual humbug, and on the book's appearance one well-known lady destroyed all the letters she had received from famous men. The *Life of Carlyle* took ten years of Froude's life and as many more of controversy. But Froude was too good an historian not to know that the finest respect to

Carlyle was to paint him warts and all; and in fact there emerged a wonderful, speaking portrait of a man of genius, with his gifts and qualities and defects. Froude thought it his best book—and an author usually knows better than anybody else whether his book is good or not. Apart from much else, it is a large slice of the intellectual history of the nineteenth century. A superb subject, with its own pathos and even dramatic interest, a mass of material of the first quality in Carlyle's own writings and letters, a subject that Froude knew well, a circle of which he was an intimate, he must have known as an artist what a masterpiece he had created.

A lesser masterpiece, but more cheerful and congenial, is Sir G. O. Trevelyan's *Life and Letters of Macaulay*. That gives you a different, though no less remarkable circle, and one that was even more at the centre of the Victorian age and its characteristic beliefs and outlook. Or for an earlier period and for a man of genius greater than any of them, more kindly, profoundly human, take Lockhart's *Life of Sir Walter Scott*—second only to Boswell's *Johnson* among English biographies. All these and many more make delightful reading, easy of approach, sympathetic in their primary interest in personality, in the story of a human being; but they are informative, directly and indirectly, of the society to which their subjects belonged and they add up to a portrait of the past which is a living possession of the present. For the past is not over and done with, but *lives* in such books. (There are plenty of books that give the impression of its being dead, but it is those books that are dead.)

The biographies of great men of action provide the most useful introductions to the periods their lives so much affected. I do not propose to enter here into the exact character of the influence of great men in history, even if it could be defined; what I have to say on the general question has been said in Chapter V. But no one can deny that, within limits, the action of a great man at a critical stage may be decisive. It is interesting to watch the difficulties that a would-be orthodox Marxist like Trotsky has in allowing for the undeniably decisive influence of Lenin in the Russian Revolution: it is the most curiously revealing part of his history of the Revolution. Yet however much the Revolution owed to Lenin, nothing would have come of him and his movement if he had not been presented with his chance in 1917. The point is that he was prepared for it and knew how to use it.

It is often, therefore, a useful way of summing up a significant theme in history to view it through the career of the man indissolubly connected with it: to see the end of the Roman Republic and the beginnings of the Empire through the life of Julius Cæsar, the Puritan Revolution and the Civil War in this country through that of Cromwell, the culmination of the French Revolution and its spirit of militant aggression in the career of Napoleon. Naturally the biography of even the most dominating of historical figures does not exhaust the interest of the theme and period: one needs to see the end of the Roman Republic through the career of Cicero as well as Cæsar, the French Revolutionary period through Robespierre as much as Napoleon.

I have already mentioned (Chapter II) the use and pleasure there are in reading history in enriching our appreciation of literature. Here I should emphasise how much of historical writing is itself good literature. When we are young we are apt to think that literature means poetry and plays, novels, short stories, essays. As we grow older we realise that history is just as much literature and the great historians are great writers as much as the poets and novelists. Perhaps history is a more mature appreciation and corresponds to a ripening of taste. Many people who liked reading novels or poetry when young come to prefer reading biography and memoirs, or letters and diaries, later on. It is easier to appreciate the *Vicar of Wakefield* than the *Decline and Fall of the Roman Empire* ; but there is no doubt which is the greater work. Clarendon is one of the greatest writers of the later seventeenth century. Hume's *History* is not unworthy of the philosopher, and brought him greater success in his own day than his philosophical writings. Or what are we to say of the rich array of historians in the nineteenth century? Carlyle, Macaulay, Froude—they are not inferior to the great novelists of that wonderfully fertile age.

Nor must we forget how many of the greatest writers whose main achievements were elsewhere have been attracted by history and made their contributions to it. Sir Thomas More wrote his life of Edward V, as Bacon his history of Henry VII. It has often been remarked how much of English history may be learned from Shakespeare's plays. Hobbes wrote his history of the Civil War, Milton his *History of Britain*. Newman wrote a good deal on the subject, Kingsley less, though his enthusiasm for the Elizabethan age—caught from his brother-in-law, Froude— is the making of *Westward Ho!* Even Dickens, least historically-minded of writers, wrote his *Child's History of England*; Thackeray, steeped in the eighteenth century, made a direct contribution with his *Four Georges*, and a far more valuable indirect one with *Henry Esmond*. When we come to Kipling and Hardy, each in his way is impregnated with the sense of history. Kipling, like Dickens, attempted a text-book history of England, though his real perception of it was imaginative and to be found in *Puck of Pook's Hill* and *Rewards and Fairies*. Though Hardy lived through the great war of 1914–1918, his mind was possessed, as T. E. Lawrence found when he visited him, by the Napoleonic War : *that* was the Great War to him, upon which his imagination brooded, to produce such masterpieces as *The Trumpet Major* and *The Dynasts*.

A knowledge of history enriches even our appreciation of music, most rarefied of the arts and the most *sui generis*. Perhaps we may return to the passage quoted on page 159 where Trevelyan says: "Music needs no such historic introduction to be fully appreciated, for it is not allusive, or only slightly." But not quite so. It is true that the appreciation of music is of its own kind, a musical experience. But over and above that, it is full of allusions, and there is always the allusion to its own time and period, of which it is the most intimate and secret revelation possible. When you listen to Bach and hear the dance-rhythms of gigue and courante, sarabande or bourrée or polonaise, it is as if you can see those figures of the eighteenth century weaving their way in and out the patterns of the dance, slow and stately, or sprightly and gay, with their low bows and curtsies, the gentlemen handing the ladies, the turns and rhythms so expressive of the equipoise, the deliberation of the age. There is a more staccato vigour, something more primitive in the jigs of the Elizabethans, a more solemn formality in their pavans. The lovely unsurpassable melodies of Schubert have a direct relation to the popular music of the Vienna of his time: it had even its response, if less direct, in the deep and philosophical spirit of Beethoven. Or how fully to appreciate the music of Palestrina without hearing

214

it, as we would see a picture by Tintoretto, springing out of its proper time and circumstance: the sixteenth century, the polyphonic tradition, the religious conflict, the Renaissance impulse passing over into the Counter-Reformation, the renewal of faith? When you realise what the submergence of the Catholic faith and its persecution under Elizabeth meant to spirits like William Byrd, the pathos and tenderness of his settings of the Mass gain a new poignancy, the asseveration of his faith a deeper meaning in the motets he wrote for the feast of Corpus Christi.

With the music of our own time the thing becomes even more subtle, as with so much of contemporary art: it often has a direct reference to the art of a previous period, sometimes springs out of its very idiom. Just as Rex Whistler's painting refers back to the Regency, or Martyn Skinner's *Letters to Malaya* to the manner of the eighteenth century, so in a still deeper way with the music of Ravel and Vaughan Williams. With Ravel, as with Prokoviev, one sometimes gets the impression of the work being *pastiche*, he had such an acute sense of period and style, and such cleverness in reproducing them: in *Pavane pour une Infante Défunte* it is the early seventeenth century, in the *Tombeau de Couperin* it is the mid-seventeenth, in *La Valse* there is a Strauss waltz of the high nineteenth century, tricked out with all the resources of the twentieth in harmony and orchestration. All the same, this was the way in which

Ravel thought: the sense of a previous period released something in him, and stimulated him to create. So too with Vaughan Williams: the music of the sixteenth century, of Tallis and Byrd, is his natural language; indeed he shares their experience: he did not come to express himself fully until he had found himself in them. With him, more than with any other composer, the language of a previous age loosened his own tongue, released a creative impulse: a nostalgic spirit, replete with the sense of history.

The experience of music is perhaps the most subtle and inward way that is left to us of experiencing any age that is gone by. In it we can still hear its pulse, listen to its heart-beats still: in nothing are we more closely in touch with its very spirit, responding too, centuries afterwards, to the passions and regrets, the joys and griefs that moved those others in their day. In music they live for us still: out of time, the timeless.

With music I have taken the case of an art in which the historical element is at its least direct and least essential. At the other end of the scale is architecture, the most historical of the arts, where history is at its most obvious : one might even regard architecture as history arrested in stone, the movement of time congealed into plastic form. For indeed at every point a building expresses the needs, the character, of its age. An old and complex building will bear the signs upon

216

it of various ages which it has lived through. I think as I write of a manor-house near Oxford which has a fragment of its medieval core; at the back it has an Elizabethan or Jacobean gable and a little seventeenth-century court; the front is plain, sober Georgian, but at one end a Regency bow-window is thrown out and at the other a Victorian conservatory. What generations of family-life, with their different circumstances and different ideas of domestic life, that agreeable *mélange* testifies to!

With a town there is infinitely greater variety. In almost any English town of any antiquity one moves easily from the Middle Ages in the parish church, elevated high above the little old houses around it, to the present day with its speaking contrast between the public buildings put up by government departments—post-offices or employment exchanges—with their excellent standards of design, traditional or modern, and the appalling confusion of modern commercial buildings: the multiple concerns, the shops and petrol-filling stations, the meanness of the houses—all without tradition or dignity, without conscience or neighbourliness, vulgar, garish, uncivilised. How much of contemporary life that reflects! On the way between one and the other you may easily pick out fragments of the sixteenth or seventeenth centuries, possibly a whole Georgian terrace or street, Regency shopfronts or decent Victorian dwellings. Or think how well a Wren city church reflects that decorous and substantial society: family-religion, the spacious pew, the seats behind for the servants, the high pulpit, the sermon a great feature of the service, morally edifying, common-sense, prosy: one almost sees it all, Pepys ogling a pretty woman in the intervals of singing lustily from his book, lending a critical ear to the sermon, his attention wandering back to the lady across the way or thinking regretfully of Prue at home.

Or consider Oxford with its accent on the Middle Ages and the seventeenth century. One can see the society of the time reflected in the development of the college parallel with that of the manor-house: the rather haphazard arrangement of the earliest medieval buildings at Merton, followed in the next century by the new model of a regular quadrangle, with an attached cloister, at New College. A century later, and the cloister is placed conveniently inside the quadrangle as at Magdalen for sheltered communication. Or one can watch the evolution of the T-shaped plan of the college chapel; or of the medieval domestic house with its hall and chambers through the Tudor and Stuart periods to the Georgian examples which have never been surpassed.

I have said little on the subject precisely because there is so much to be said about it: many books have been written on the history of architecture and on the relations of the two. History is the front-door approach to architecture,

218

and almost every historian who is any good is keenly interested in it. The interest in these things and the pleasure they give are inexhaustible. For the reader's guidance I would suggest a little Victorian book that is still useful, Parker's *A.B.C. of Gothic Architecture* and some such introduction as W. R. Lethaby's *Architecture* or W. H. Godfrey's *Story of English Architecture*. From these you may pass on to such a fine work as E. S. Prior's *History of Gothic Art in England* or Willis and Clark's masterpiece, *The Architectural History of the University of Cambridge*, in which virtually the whole of English architecture is reflected in that mirror. Who will write a similar *magnum opus* for Oxford? A masterpiece is waiting to be written.

To judge only from the letters that reach me, there are very many people in the country who derive great pleasure from family history, particularly from the history of their own family. It is a harmless form of snobbery and a pleasant pursuit. I cannot analyse its pleasures here, but they have an excellent foundation in their appeal to vanity—particularly, I note, to male vanity, whether in men or in masculine ladies—than which there can be no more solid or permanent foundation for pleasure. The interest in the family is a prime extension of the ego: what more appealing to us mortals? Naturally if it is to come up to scratch and yield satisfaction it must be an old family going back a good long way, the older and more devious the better. It does not need to have been a great family, important politically, like Cecils or Howards or Russells, though such families are of more interest to the historian. To the amateur—I use the word in its literal sense—the pursuit is all the better for being not too easy, a little difficult and obscure: more fun in the dark. But the older the family the more scope it gives: the more wills to be tracked down, with their delightful, tantalising references to heirlooms and treasures all too probably vanished —but think of the amusement of recognising them still there in a chest or jewel-box after the centuries! And the more references in parish registers to be sought out and sifted: it is all the better if the family-tree is not too erect—a little bastardy here and there adds to its interest. There are people altruistic enough to take an interest in other people's families; if you have no family of your own to speak of, there is an alternative. It may provide a bottom for a lasting interest in history: after all, human society consists of families.

The interest in family history is bound up with so many other delightful things: the interest of the old house in which so much has taken place, the charm of its possessions, pictures, hangings, furniture, down to the maps of the estate, the stories of its ghosts. It extends to all the locality; and as Dr. J. H. Weaver tells us, there is no end to local history: "The material of local history, in the broad sense of the word, is almost unlimited in quantity, or limited only by what is actually available in our national records as a whole." As you see, it conforms at least to the second half of that excellent definition of a hobby—'has no sense at all and no finality.'

It leads straight to the pleasures of archæologising, of pick and shovel, the esoteric excitements of the dig. Or perhaps they are not so esoteric after all: they go back to the primitive enjoyment of the treasure-hunt. Most of us share readily in the fun of a picnic-jaunt across moor and cliff in all weathers, mackintosh and sou'-wester if necessary, to cliff-camp or dolmen, to stone-circle or barrow, or some Wayland Smith's cave on the downs. Walking is best, map in hand; sandwiches must not be forgotten: they taste better out in the open air after a long tramp. Nor must we forget that archæology, more than any other branch of historical study, provides scope for the pleasures of hatred, malice and all uncharitableness. Anybody who knows the ways of county antiquaries knows that *odium theologicum* is nothing compared with *odium archæologicum*.

A fascinating subject that has been opened up only in our own time, and in which already enormous strides have been made, is the study of English place-names. It adds to the pleasure of walking the countryside to know the derivation and meaning of the names of places you go through: often they throw a shaft of light into the most distant past and will reveal to you the nature and origin of the place, its early settlement, the character of the whole district. So much of the documentation of our early history has perished: the place-names themselves are the most reliable documents that remain. Here you may come upon a Celtic name that reveals to you an early British settlement that went on happily among the surrounding English. There are many Waltons in various parts of the country, often, though not always, meaning just that: Welsh-towns. Or take the little finger of Saxon names along the river Ottery on the Cornish side of the Tamar pointing into that almost completely Celtic county: surviving evidence of an English settlement on that side of the border. The study of the place-names of Devon has revealed, what we should not have known otherwise, that it was settled by West Saxons coming in from the north, from Somerset, not, as we should have supposed, from Dorset coming straight west along the coast. It does not count for nothing in their subsequent character and history that Devon and Somerset are more English and less Celtic than Dorset. Or take Cumberland and Westmorland: their place-names will reveal to you the fact that their population springs from a mixture of Celts, Angles, Norse, with the last possibly the dominant strain: hence that magnificent, tough, rugged stock: the dalesmen. Of such is the incomparably rich and fertile variousness of our people made.

Those great scholars Henry Bradley (read his masterly little book, *The Making of English*) and Walter Skeat were the founders of this study at the beginning of this century. In our time it has grown into a whole province of its own, in which the *gauleiter* are Sir Allen Mawer and Professor F. M. Stenton with a distinguished recruit from Scandinavia—where there is great interest in the study and whence some of the most valuable contributions have come—Professor Eilert Ekwall. There is a society, the English Place-Name Society, devoted to it, engaged in surveying the whole country, county by county, giving a volume to each, sometimes more. You should make a point of looking up your own county in the series; if it has not yet appeared there may be another book that covers it: many counties have been dealt with. Then read the Introductory volume to the Survey, which gives you an admirable guide to the subject and its methods. One cannot hope, alas, to purchase all the volumes of the Survey; but in default of that, there is an excellent alternative: *The Concise Oxford Dictionary of English Place-Names* (by Professor Ekwall).

Some people derive pleasure from military history or naval. These are rarer; but a great many more are equipped to study and understand it now. Besides the biographical and political interest it shares with general history—the excitement of such characters as Alexander the Great, Julius Cæsar and Napoleon, Marlborough,

Wellington, Nelson—it has special grounds of appeal: the interest in geography, in roads and communications, in strategy, tactics, logistics, even in the weather. Rarer still are those who find pleasure in the history of theological doctrines —a leading pursuit in previous centuries, now much on the wane. It is questionable whether one ought to discourage any form of intellectual interest: however pointless in itself, it may yield lights on other subjects. I must however issue a warning: Burckhardt tells us that Buckle's intensive study of the Scotch divines of the seventeenth century cost him his paralysis of the brain.

In the end, as always in history, we come back to that experience we call the 'moment of illumination.' It is nowhere better described than by Browning:

On the arch where olives overhead
    Print the blue sky with twig and leaf
(That sharp-curled leaf which they never shed)
    Twixt the aloes, I used to lean in chief,
And mark through the winter afternoons,
    By a gift God grants me now and then,
In the mild decline of those suns like moons,
    Who walked in Florence, besides her men.

Chapter Eight

How to Teach Yourself History

YOU might think that in order to learn history you need a library of books to begin with. But not at all: that only comes at the end. What you need at the beginning is a pair of stout walking shoes, a pencil and a notebook; perhaps I should add a good county guide covering the area you mean to explore—I find Methuen's *Little Guides* most useful—and a map of the country, preferably a one-inch Ordnance Survey that gives you field footpaths and a wealth of things of interest, marks churches and historic buildings and ruins, wayside crosses and holy wells, prehistoric camps and dykes, the sites of battles. When you can't go for a walk it is quite a good thing to study the map and plan where you would like to go. I am all in favour of the open-air approach to history: the most delightful and enjoyable, the most imaginative and informative, and— what not everybody understands—the best training.

This is the true countryman's approach, and it has great advantages, especially in understanding the early history of the island. You might take Jacquetta Hawkes' delightful little book *Early Britain* (Collins' *Britain in Pictures* series), with its

beautiful illustrations, and graduate from that to
V. Gordon Childe's *Prehistoric Communities of the
British Isles*. The first of these is enough to equip
you to tackle the prehistoric ridgeways and tracks
that exist all over the country and offer the best
walking, springy turf, air like wine, a blessed
release from the noise and traffic of the modern
world—only the larks and occasionally (alas!)
the planes. The distinguished archæologist, Dr.
O. G. S. Crawford, tells us that countrymen understand best, almost instinctively, the conditions of
prehistoric life, and that the proceedings of small
country field-clubs are often far ahead of the
leading archæological journals in the true appreciation of prehistoric problems. This is the man who
in our time has demonstrated by air-photography
the Celtic system of agriculture, with its small fields
on the uplands, that was brought to an end by the
English who cleared the forests and river valleys.
You can still see the traces of that earlier upland
cultivation revealed in the air photographs. (Look
them up in that most agreeable journal, *Antiquity*.)

I do not know if you realise that in prehistoric
times the whole country was covered with a
system of upland communications: "The ridgeways and harrow-ways that connected the hill-top
forts and the Celtic villages formed a system of
communications the excellence of which we are
only now beginning to appreciate." So Mr.
Randall in his *History in the Open Air*; his essay on
"The Old Roads of England" is an excellent aid

to a good road-sense: I mean, of course, an historic sense of the road, not just how to drive a car. He shows us how to keep a weather-eye open, for "an existing bit of road may be partly prehistoric, partly Roman, partly medieval and partly modern"; and he gives us two valuable clues to follow: "the capital distinction is between the roads that grew and the roads that were made. . . . Secondly, the age of a road is determined by the earliest monuments or objects found in definite relation to it." Mr. Belloc, of whom I do not approve as an historian—he is so full of prejudice and *parti pris*—nevertheless has a fine sense of topography and an eye for the road; and I recommend his account of the old Pilgrims' road to Canterbury, *The Old Road*, in spite of its mistakes, as an example of the right approach and the right feeling for roads—moreover by a man of genius with a gift of style.

There ought to be similar books for our waterways—rivers and canals. What delightful books are waiting to be written in this field, or, perhaps I should say, in these waters. So far as the rivers are concerned, the emphasis might be on the Middle Ages and the medieval towns along their routes. Mr. Randall tells us: "The Thames is navigable at least to Lechlade, and before the digging of the canals it was navigable to Cricklade. From these points the journey over the Cotswold country to the Severn, or either of the Avons, would be a matter of two or three days even for fairly heavy loads. It is sometimes made a matter of wonder how goods were transported along foundrous medieval roads in cumbersome medieval carts. The answer is that for the most part they went by water." Here too we have a guide in Mr. Belloc's *Historic Thames*, and a model for what may be done for other rivers, Severn and Trent, Tyne and Tees and the various Avons. We have a classic canal-book in Stevenson's *An Inland Voyage*. To the pleasures of walking we add those of canoeing and exploring our waterways by steamer and barge and boat. Nor are the railways—most characteristic product of the high Industrial Revolution—without their historic interest. I suggest as an introduction C. E. R. Sherrington's *A Hundred Years of Inland Transport*, from which one may rise to a full-dress history like W. W. Tomlinson's *History of the North-Eastern Railway*. Railways have their fans—and their fascination—no less than roads and rivers.

The townsman too has his advantages, especially if, as is usually the case in this country, he lives in an old town, or a town that still has something old about it: if he keeps his eyes open there is more for him to see—more, I mean, that is worth seeing. Most English towns of any size have had books written about them that will serve as guides to their past and tell you what there is of interest in them: inquire at the local library or bookshop, particularly if the latter is an old business going back several generations. Nothing more delightful to discover in a town—one of the pleasures of going to a country town is searching out and savouring the local bookshops: there is as much art in it as in wine-tasting. But I must draw your attention to an enchanting introduction to *English Cities and Small Towns* by a writer of originality and talent, John Betjeman. Everything by this writer is to be read, thought over and absorbed: his books are brief, but they are the works of a poet with an acute sense of the past and an infallible eye. Read also his *Vintage London* and *An Oxford University Chest*. There is an admirable old *Historic Towns* series to pick up second-hand: edited by the historian Freeman, one of whose strongest points was his sense of topography. (His travel sketch-books of towns abroad, in Normandy and Maine, in Provence and Sicily, are the most agreeable things that rather disagreeable old person ever wrote.) Or take as an example of the method to follow in studying an historic town a recent book: *English City: The Growth and Future of Bristol*. (University of London Press.) With the aid of a book like that you get an idea of the layout and growth of a city, its vital parts and organic functions: the place begins to come clear to your mind and to live for you as a place, with a personality of its own, complex and satisfying, no longer a mere passive, unnoticed background to the squalid life of the ignorant destined to quick oblivion.

So too for our counties with their wonderful

diversity of character and inexhaustible treasures of interest. One of the greatest things about this country—it is hardly more realised at home than it is abroad—is the infinite diversity it presents within the smallest possible space. Oxford stands at the gates of four quite different landscapes, itself characteristic of a fifth: the wooded slopes of the Chilterns, the bare lines of the Berkshire downs, the Cotswold uplands and valleys, the quiet rolling country of North Oxfordshire; the city itself a Thames valley town. In a large continental country like the United States or Russia or Australia, you may travel for hundreds of miles with hardly a change of feature in the landscape: how boring! The only thing for it is a plane. An enduring feature in English history is the difference between one county and another —the "coloured counties" indeed! Think of the extraordinary differences between next-door neighbours, in temperament, dialect, character of the people, landscape, between Cornwall and Devon, Devon and Dorset, Dorset and Wilts and so through all the southern counties; or between Lancashire and Yorkshire, Cumberland and Northumberland. Anyone who is to understand England must understand this, in addition to the fact that in these islands there are four different countries: England, Wales, Scotland, Ireland. Most fortunate diversity, chief source of our inexhaustible creativeness! Greece was the most diverse country of the ancient world.

In addition to Methuen's *Little Guides* to the counties, there is an Oxford series of *County Histories* intended for schools, now out of print. It should be revived and brought up to date; much more should be made of county history in the schools. An admirable example of how it should be done is Mr. Alec Macdonald's *Worcestershire in English History*. From these popular introductory works one can move on to magnificent quarries of material and information: to the *Victoria County Histories*, for example, of which we may cite that of Lancashire as a model and the most complete. Then there are the superb volumes, with their illustrations, of the Historical Monuments Commission: surveys of the country, county by county, with all that is of archæological and historical interest in them. The one really serious defect of the scheme is that they stop short at 1714. This should be remedied and the volumes pressed on with as soon as possible—before another war comes along to destroy yet more of our heritage from the past. Meanwhile there is an admirable little series of *Regional Guides* to Ancient Monuments in the care of the Ministry of Works (Stationery Office). From all this one may move back—or on—to the older standard histories of the counties, of which we may cite Hoare's *Wiltshire* and Ormerod's *Cheshire* as classic examples. An additional allurement is the characteristic engravings and prints with which these older volumes are embellished:

satisfying and agreeable in themselves, they are often of houses, alas! now vanished or of views all too disagreeably changed. Many counties have their own archæological and historical societies, with Journals and Proceedings that have been going for many years and contain a great deal of valuable and fascinating material. Let me cite only the *Transactions of the Devonshire Association* as a good example. Other societies exist to publish chiefly documents, like the Oxford Historical Society, or, for the North Country, the Surtees and Chetham Societies.

But this is not intended to become a bibliography. The National Book League exists to publish bibliographies, among other things; it has recently issued an admirable Book-list (No. 149) on "British Civilisation and Institutions," in itself an excellent practical guide to English history. Mr. Watkin Davies' book *How to Read History* (Hodder & Stoughton) is a very useful guide, if a little out of date, to reading on general history. My object is to explain, simply and briefly, how best to teach yourself history.

There are three golden rules, it seems to me:

1. KEEP YOUR EYES OPEN.
2. TAKE NOTES.
3. READ THE RIGHT BOOKS.

The first of these I have dealt with. The second implies the third, and I must explain the art of taking notes. It is not only from books that one takes notes; one may take notes from lectures, or notes of things seen or observed. The point is that if you are to teach yourself history you should always have a notebook at hand, or carry a small one in your pocket. Into that you enter the things of interest you want to remember: it may be an inscription on a monument, or useful date (there has been nothing in this book about dates, that boring bugbear of the anti-historical), a building or some object you may want to know more about or of which you want to remember the appearance; or it may be the name of a book, a quotation, or some passage you fancy; or a note of some portrait or picture in a gallery. (Get into the habit of visiting picture galleries and museums when you can: they give an interesting slant on history, their contents are part of the life of the past, so much treasure-trove cast up by the tide of time.)

The art of taking notes from lectures is the same as that of making notes from books: the salient point is to get down the gist of the thing. It is possible to take too many notes: Lord Acton took so many that he never could get on with his writing, and his famous Inaugural Lecture is a nightmare of quotations: it makes one feel that at some time or other someone has thought of everything. What you will find is that at the beginning of your reading you will need to take more notes than later on. At first a great deal of what you read will be new to you and you will want to memorise it; later on, as your reading grows, the picture will fill in for you: partly consciously and partly unconsciously, a deposit of knowledge will accumulate and you will need to take fewer notes: you will already know something of what you are reading and will need to note only what is new. On the basis of what you have read before *plus* your own sense, you may be able in time to criticise what you are reading. At the beginning it is a good idea to try to summarise the gist of each paragraph of what you are reading into one sentence, or at most two; and in addition to take down any striking passage or phrase you may want to quote *verbatim*.

A word on the books you should read. *It is most important always to read the best books you can on a subject.* Beginners hardly realise how important this is; but you may be given quite a wrong view of a subject by starting off on the wrong footing. Most of the ridiculous nonsense that is talked about history by people who don't know comes from their reading trash on the subject. Take, for example, the absurd (and rather obscene) popular ideas about Henry VIII and Queen Elizabeth: you should read A. F. Pollard's biography of Henry, not Francis Hackett's; J. E. Neale's *Queen Elizabeth* and Milton Waldman's *Elizabeth and Leicester*, not Belloc's or Theodore Maynard's stuff about her. It is here that tutors and lecturers can be most useful, in putting you on to the best books to read: after all, the reading you must do for yourself. But if you are very much on your own, as most people are, there is no reason to be downcast or despairing; for once you get on the track of the right reading, you will build up a critical knowledge for yourself that will tell you what is sense and what is nonsense.

It may be thought that I have lost sight of the history of the country as such. Not at all; I have had it in mind all the time. As I have said, the mental world of the average, even intelligent, man is largely limited to his own country: he does not enter intimately or in any significant way into the languages and cultures of others. The history of his own country therefore has a central importance and he needs to begin by getting an adequate picture of that. Perhaps I may be forgiven for suggesting my *Spirit of English History* as an introduction, since it is the briefest possible. It is only an introduction, intended as a summing up of what our history comes to and to show how it has developed on the lines it has, so differently from other people's. It must be followed by a book on a bigger scale with more scope for detailed treatment; the best is G. M. Trevelyan's *History of England*. This may be accompanied by J. A. Williamson's *The Evolution of England* or A. F. Pollard's *History of England*; but it should be followed by Williamson's *Great Britain and the Empire*. Arrived at this point one can fill out the picture with Trevelyan's *English Social History*, and W. J. Ashley's *The Economic Organisation of England*; and embark safely on a work of genius, with all its faults and in spite of its being gloriously out of date, in Green's *Short History of the English People*.

You might think it safe to launch out now on the classics of historical writing, Macaulay, Carlyle, Froude; Clarendon, Hume, Gibbon. But not quite yet. These for the most part deal with definite periods; and it is better perhaps to get an idea of those periods in terms of modern scholarship first: you will get things in a better perspective, be able to discount their bias, note their prejudices and avoid their mistakes. For example, for the sixteenth century you should read Fisher's and Pollard's volumes in Longmans' History of England, together with Neale's *Elizabeth* and Williamson's *The Age of Drake*. Then you can go on to Froude's *History of England*. Similarly for the seventeenth century: first read Trevelyan's *England under the Stuarts*, G. N. Clark's *The Later Stuarts* in the new Oxford History of England and Trevelyan's *England under Queen Anne*; then go on to Macaulay.

This may be thought to be timid counsel, for, after all, the great historians have far more to offer in the end than lesser writers: imaginative power, literary gifts that enable them to re-create where others just plod along after the facts, a deeper insight into the ways of men, more knowledge of the world—in a word, genius. Nor are they ever afraid to say what they think: they must—or bust. But I am only providing here for the beginner; later on he will be able to read the classics with all the more understanding. At the beginning he needs someone to warn him as to the particular bias and prejudices of a given writer.

Take, for example, the greatest of English historians, Gibbon. He has two grave defects. He can never do justice to Christianity and what it did achieve—the civilisation of the barbarians, for one thing. Because he could not accept its supernatural, and indeed irrational, claims, the author of *The Decline and Fall of the Roman Empire* seizes every opportunity to denigrate the Church and its adherents and to present them in a ridiculous light: the book is full of sly remarks, subacid inflections, dubious jokes, pin-pricks. Very amusing, very naughty; but strictly from an historian's point of view, rather shocking. He ought to have been fair and impartial, whereas with him the case—and the joke—always goes against the Christians. Personally I share his fundamental standpoint, the rejection of their supernatural claims; but not to appreciate their good work in the world, along with the bad, the marvellous achievements of the Church along with its failures and misdeeds, is in itself unhistorical. Then, too, he is very unjust to the Byzantine Empire, which represents a remarkable positive achievement that Gibbon seems to have been unaware of: for a thousand years it stood on guard at the gate of European civilisation against the Turks, and even then would never have fallen if it had not been irretrievably weakened by the disgraceful onslaught of the West in the Latin Crusade. Gibbon was obsessed—not unreasonably perhaps—by the folly of mankind: he thought that history "is, indeed, little more than the register of the crimes, follies, and misfortunes of mankind." But this is only one side of the picture: too much of the great canvas he painted is in eighteenth-century chiaroscuro. He had no sense of the spiritual achievement of man; his vision of the world has something in common with Swift's. But that is only to say that he was the child of his age, of that age of enlightenment, of scepticism and disillusion. All the same, his defects are nothing compared with his gifts and qualities: to read him is an education in itself.

With a general picture of English history in mind, you can then branch out in two directions. On the one hand you can follow up the periods and subjects of English history that interest you in greater detail; on the other you can make it your aim to get some idea of general European history. Once you have gone a certain way with the latter and got a firm outline in mind, it is a good thing to work the two together to some extent. Let me make this clear by illustration. H. A. L. Fisher's *History of Europe* will give you a good outline of the story of European civilisation from ancient Greece onwards: probably the most convenient introduction, liberal, old-fashioned, humane. I think it desirable also to get the hang of prehistory: read Sir John Myres' brilliant little book, *The Dawn of History*, and two of Gordon Childe's, *Man Makes Himself* and *What Happened in History*. You might follow these with one or two books that cover whole periods: Warde Fowler's *Rome*, H. W. C. Davis' *Medieval Europe*, Bryce's *Holy Roman Empire*, G. N. Clark's *The Seventeenth Century*, Bertrand Russell's *Freedom and Organisation in the Nineteenth Century*. Then you can go in more detail into some particular period. I agree with Bury's view that it is practically more important for people to know about the most recent period of history, that which provides the background to events today, which has such a dominating influence upon our own lives. It is here that the two strands come together: while you are reading English history you must see it in relation to the European and world environment.

The last volume in the new Oxford History, R. C. K. Ensor's *England 1870–1914*, is a first-class survey of the events leading up to our own time: stimulating at every point, very wide in its sympathies, fresh-minded and original. No one could possibly find history anything but fascinating if written like that. Or, for the whole century, there is Trevelyan's *British History in the Nineteenth Century*. But these books telling us what was happening here should be read along with those describing events abroad, both in Europe and beyond. For France, read D. W. Brogan's *The Development of Modern France*; for Germany, A. J. P. Taylor's *The Course of German History*; both independent-minded, trenchant, thought-provoking. For Russia, read B. H. Sumner's *Survey of Russian History*, rather more difficult, for it is an original attempt at a new method, to read history back from the situation today; but a strikingly impartial treatment of a notoriously controversial subject. For the United States, read Allan Nevins' excellent and concise *Brief History of the United States* and go on to Morison and Commager's *The Growth of the American Republic*. For the European background as a whole I might suggest Croce's *History of Europe in the Nineteenth Century*, and Alison Phillips' *Modern Europe*. The two strands may be usefully brought together in R. W. Seton-Watson's *Britain in Europe, 1789–1914*.

From now on, with such a general framework of history in mind, you will be able to fill it out wherever you choose, in the most congenial manner possible, by reading historical biographies. With such a firm framework to go upon there will be no danger of getting them out of chronological order, or out of proportion in the general perspective. In any case there is a remedy: to read biographies on both sides of historic conflicts, Strafford as well as Cromwell, Gladstone as well as Disraeli, Stalin *and* Trotsky. Let me give a few examples only of the biographical approach. Let us take Napoleon. You could not do better than begin with H. A. L. Fisher's brilliant little *Napoleon*, and go on to Fournier's standard biography in two volumes. But you should get the point of view of his critics and opponents too: read also, therefore, Duff-Cooper's *Talleyrand*, Algernon Cecil's *Metternich*, Holland Rose's *Life of William Pitt*; then go on to Mathiez' *History of the French Revolution* and J. M. Thompson's *French Revolution*. In the end you should graduate with Sorel's great classic, *L'Europe et la Révolution Française*.

Or again for the English nineteenth century, you might begin with Lytton Strachey's *Queen Victoria*, Philip Guedalla's *The Duke* and his *Palmerston*, and go on to G. M. Young's *Early Victorian England*, Monypenny and Buckle's *Disraeli* and Morley's *Gladstone*.

But this is becoming too much of a bibliography; my excuse is that these are only illustrations of the method of historical reading. And I think I have indicated enough to start you off on your way: you should be able to go forward on your own steam now. These books will have their own bibliographies and references to other books in which to follow up what interests you. And you will by now have developed, almost unconsciously, a critical sense that will help you to pick and choose. This will be needed when you come to tackle large works of corporate scholarship like the Cambridge Histories, Ancient, Medieval and Modern, the Cambridge History of the British Empire, of British Foreign Policy and so on. For the most important fact about these works is that you are not expected to read them right through—nobody could—but to pick out the chapters that are germane to your subject: they differ very much in quality. In fact you have learnt to *use* books as well as to read them for pleasure.

Looking out for the books you want is itself a pleasure, occasionally heightened by expectancy and sharpened by irritation at not finding what one wants. The delights of book-collecting are well known and have often been celebrated. What more agreeable pursuit than bookshop-crawling? A more varied and complex pleasure than the other, for which one has so much more to show in the end: a well-stocked library and, I hope, a well-stocked mind.

As for historical research, in the pure sense of the word, I have said little of it directly, for that is a subject of its own, of a specialist character. And there are various standard works to which you can refer, covering the subject—such as Langlois and Seignobos' *Introduction to the Study of History* and C. G. Crump's *History and Historical Research*. There is an admirable series of S.P.C.K. pamphlets too, "Helps for Students of History," now unfortunately out of print, but sometimes obtainable second-hand. On the subject of writing history I have said nothing at all: for its pleasures and excitements, rare and esoteric, simple and satisfying, I refer you to that revealing masterpiece, Gibbon's *Autobiography*.

Note on Books

A GOOD many books are referred to, and quoted from, in the course of this book. The following may be found particularly useful.

C. H. WILLIAMS (ed.), *The Modern Historian* (Nelson), 1938.

H. WATKIN-DAVIES, *How to Read History* (Hodder & Stoughton), 1924.

F. J. WEAVER, *The Material of English History* (Nelson), 1938.

G. M. TREVELYAN, *The Recreations of an Historian* (Nelson), 1919.

Sir CHARLES OMAN, *On the Writing of History* (Methuen), 1939.

H. BUTTERFIELD, *The Englishman and his History*, (Cambridge U.P.), 1944.

J. B. BURY, *Selected Essays* (Cambridge U.P.), 1930.

G. P. GOOCH, *History and Historians in the Nineteenth Century* (Longmans), 1913.

J. B. BLACK, *The Art of the Historian* (Methuen).

C. G. CRUMP, *History and Historical Research* (Routledge), 1928.

M. W. KEATINGE, *Studies in the Teaching of History* (Black), 1913.

J. BURCKHARDT, *Reflections on History* (Allen & Unwin), 1943.

H. A. HODGES, *Wilhelm Dilthey: An Introduction* (Kegan Paul), 1944.

THE USE OF HISTORY

CH. V. LANGLOIS and CH. SEIGNOBOS: *Introduction to the Study of History* (Duckworth), 1898.

C. JOHNSON and J. P. WHITNEY (ed.), *Helps for Students of History* (S.P.C.K.), 1918, 1919.

The following periodicals:
History. Published by Macmillan & Co.
Antiquity. Published by Roland Austin, 24, Parkend Road, Gloucester.

For more detailed research read :
The English Historical Review (Longmans).
The Economic History Review (A. & C. Black).
The Antiquaries' Journal (Oxford University Press).

Readers are recommended to join the Historical Association, 29, Gordon Square, London, W.C.1, and their own local or county antiquarian society.

Index

INDEX